OTHER BOOKS BY MARY ETHEL ECKARD

The Making of a Dragonfly,
Following Christ Through the Winds of Change
(Available through Amazon)

In the Stillness,
A Journal of Quiet Time Reflection
Dragonfly Ministries
(Available through Amazon)

Lessons of a DRAGONFLY

Forty Days to a Transformed Life

MARY ETHEL ECKARD

Lessons of a Dragonfly
Forty Days to a Transformed Life
Mary Ethel Eckard

Published by

Mary Ethel

Mary Ethel Eckard
Frisco, Texas

Cover Design | JOSEP Designs

To contact the author
www.maryetheleckard.com

ISBN (Print): 978-1-7338233-0-2
ISBN (Ebook): 978-1-7338233-1-9

Lessons of a Dragonfly, Forty Days to a Transformed Life
Winner of Christian Literary Awards 2019 Henri Award recipient,
Receiving the Seal of Excellence Medallion.

Finalist in the 2020 Next Generation Indie Awards,
Christian Non-Fiction category.

CONTENTS

DEDICATION

To my children. Aubrey, Kendall and
Jon, Tyler and Miranda, and Patrick Daniel.
To my grandchildren. Luke, Logan, Elyana,
Noah, Lily, Abram, Leah, and Simeon.
You light up my life. Your unconditional love and support sustain me.

To my parents, Elsie and Johnny, and to my
siblings, Vicki, Sandra and John.
You are the family that built me and keeps me foundationally grounded.

To my dragonflies and friends around the world. Your love
and prayers have greatly enhanced my life and calling. Never
underestimate the power of prayer and bearing the burdens
of one another. God's light shines through your testimony.
Embrace the privilege of spending quiet time with Him.
He alone transforms character and creates life out of our darkness.

You have each blessed me immeasurably with your
love and prayers. To God be the glory!

"The Lord bless you and keep you;
the Lord make His face shine upon you and be gracious to you;
the Lord turn His face toward you and give you peace."
Numbers 6:24-26

FOREWORD

Two sisters and a brother captured the heart of Jesus and they captured His. They knew Him, they walked with Him, they served Him, ate with Him, laughed with Him, cried with Him, learned from Him, were transformed by Him, captured by Him and loved Him deeply. And oh, how He loved His Lazarus, Martha and Mary. Mary is best known in the scriptures for being the one who sat at the feet of Jesus. She savored every sacred word spoken from the Lord's lips.

Here we are a couple thousand years later, still striving to follow the example of Mary who was so captivated by Jesus nothing else mattered. She longed to be in His presence, ear bent to His life-giving words, heart surrendered to His will and defended by the King of Kings for "choosing what was better." Scripture states it this way, "*There is only one thing worth being concerned about. Mary has discovered it, and it will not be taken away from her*" (Luke 10:42, NLT).

Meet my modern-day Mary, *Mary Ethel Eckard*. From the first time I met Mary, I saw Jesus flooding out of her being. I knew right away this Mary had also learned to sit at the Lord's feet and listen to Him. "I better hang around this gal," I thought, "for she has learned to tune into the whispers of the Father, the secrets of a Savior and the companionship of the Spirit." My friend Mary has taught me what it looks like to sit at the feet of Jesus and be mesmerized by His love. We have served and shared a lot of life together. I have seen her relentless pursuit of our Beloved Savior through all the joys and sorrows life brings.

Years ago, to extend a touch of God's presence to others, Mary began the practice of writing personalized prayers to everyone attending a Dragonfly Ministries retreat weekend. These prayers were breathed by the Holy Spirit, penned by Mary, and presented to retreat attendees to carry into their quiet time with the Savior.

I have been a recipient of Mary's hand-written prayers and wondered, "How did she know this is exactly the cup of cool water my parched soul needs?" She's not magical. She has trained herself to be still in the Lord's presence and listen – really listen. She speaks with the confidence and assuredness of a Princess who knows the faithfulness of her King and Heavenly Father. Those sweet prayers have bathed my soul on more than one occasion and those carefully chosen words, prayed on my behalf, could have only come from the God who is "intimately acquainted with all my ways" (Psalm 139:3).

After reading her forty days of prayers on social media, I encouraged Mary to compile them for us pilgrims who can sometimes find ourselves on the journey without words to pray. Her prayers are powerful, her posture is surrendered to His purposes, and her heart longs to invite us to discover He still listens, and He still intercedes and responds to the cries of our heart, even when those cries are silent and mere words fail.

As you read the following pages, don't be in a hurry like Martha, whose mind was preoccupied with many things. Rather, take on the character of Mary. Sit, savor, and search with all your heart the unsearchable riches of our knowable and personal God!

Let the Holy Spirit speak to you through the carefully crafted prayers and stories from "my calloused knees, tuned-in, tender-hearted prayer warrior friend," *Mary.*

Kelly Willie, Kelly Willie Ministries
Author of *"With Us, Everyday Evidence of God's Presence"*
Recording Artist, Worship Leader

FOREWORD

This forty-day devotional, written to encourage, uplift, sanctify, and bless is a comforting read that will teach you biblical lessons according to the scriptures, as well as delight you in the accompanying stories.

Mary's stories bear real-life application that we, too, can align with our everyday lives. We learn, through the pages of this book, God is for us, in us, and with us. No matter where we are, God is always there; only a prayer away, a trusted friend, companion, and one who is intensely interested in our lives. Best of all, He loves us with a love that will never be taken away, and as *Lessons of a Dragonfly* clearly illustrates, God has our back, as Protector, Leader, and Teacher He has always been, and always will be.

It is my prayer your mind and heart remain open to the lessons illustrated in this book, that serve a Godly purpose. That whomsoever is reading learns more about God's ways, thoughts, and how His intentions are toward all of us, to make us prosper. As long as we put Him first in our lives, all things will continually be added unto us, as He continues to bless each one of us according to His riches in Glory.

May you, too, take away a daily blessing and lesson from each of the stories.

Hearts Blessing
Author of https://thestagesandlessonsofmidlife.org

DRAGONFLY SYMBOLISM

The dragonfly is a symbol of growth and development. She is her strongest when she stays close to her source of strength, the sunlight. As she absorbs warmth from the sun, she reflects it through her wings for the world to see.

We are much like the dragonfly, created to grow and develop into all God has purposed. We are our strongest and best when we stay close to our source of strength, the Son light. As we absorb His light, His Holy Spirit teaches, guides, and shines through us so others are drawn to Him.

The dragonfly serves to remind us that we, too, can reflect the light of Christ in a darkened world by letting His Son shine through us.

Will you be a dragonfly for God?

> *"For God, who said, 'Let light shine out of darkness,' made his light shine in our hearts to give us the light of knowledge of the glory of God in the face of Christ."*
> 2 Corinthians 4:6

www.dragonflyministries.com

DRAGONFLY SYMBOLISM

INTRODUCTION

"I will betroth you to me forever." Hosea 2:19

My first book, *The Making of a Dragonfly | Following Christ Through the Winds of Change,* was not the book I originally set out to write. However, as I leaned into God for direction in what to include, I sensed He wanted me to share my personal journey of walking through the winds of change. In that book, I share the account of brokenness that almost crushed and rendered me lifeless. My heart was raw and tender. I was buried under fear, rejection, abandonment, insignificance and insecurities, struggling to find my way out of the rubble to catch a breath. The book journeys through grief to God's promise of healing and restoration. It speaks of a life filled with love and betrayal, obedience and rebellion, heartbreak and joy.

What was the book I intended to write? Well, it is this book, *Lessons of a Dragonfly.* Throughout the healing process, in the hardest of places, I found the sweetest presence of the Holy Spirit who held and sustained me with the gentlest of words. He led me into the wilderness;[1] not to a place of punishment, but to a place of solitude, comfort, and healing. A place I could sit at His feet, ask questions, and seek understanding.[2] He gave me the grace of time to process through my grief and pain. He opened my eyes to see how He took the scars of my wounds and turned them into beauty marks of His love. He engraved His name on my heart, so I will never again fight the battle of being not-enough or less-than.[3]

Being in the wilderness with God brought me to new life. He called me out of the tomb of brokenness and placed me in the womb of His love. "Mary, my beloved, come forth to new life." I shook off the grave clothes and walked into a spacious world where I have freedom in Him. I worry less about what others think of me, as I have learned to be true to myself. That is the work of God. It took pain, despair, and grief to bring me to a place where I found healing and discovered the immeasurable, unconditional love of God.

The stories in this book lead up to and chronicle my life through the wilderness. As I leaned into knowing God intimately, He showed me life through His lens and from His perspective. These are the life-changing stories He used to captivate my heart, teach me His ways, and mesmerize me by His love. My prayer is that these same stories will call you deeper into the heart of God, and you will desire to sit at His feet, and know Him from the inside out.

As you embark on this forty-day journey, allow time to scribe your thoughts and prayers in the space provided. Included at the end of each devotion are questions to consider as well as additional scripture references. I suggest finding these verses and writing them in the margin next to their place of reference (within the devotional). This will be helpful in scripture application as well as navigating through the Bible.

Whether you are recovering from a broken and raw heart or you are in preparation for days ahead, this book provides insight and wisdom. May the Lord guide and fill you with His breath as you read, journal, and pray during these next forty days. He extends the invitation, "Come."

PRAYER

Father,

You hold our lives in the palm of Your hand. Hold us steady as we embark on a journey of prayer and devotion, desiring to draw near to You. Open our ears to hear Your promptings, our heart to understand Your scripture, and our eyes to see You in the comings and goings of life. Let our desire be for You alone. Amen.

SCRIPTURE FOR DEEPER INSIGHT

[1] Hosea 2:14
[2] Luke 10:39
[3] Isaiah 44:5

REFLECTIONS

Why do you feel drawn to this forty-day journey?

Have you had a wilderness experience where the only comfort found was sitting at the feet of Jesus? What did you learn about God during this time? (Example: He is Comforter, Friend, a great listener.)

Day One

<hr/>

FORTY DAYS TO A TRANSFORMED LIFE

"With your help, I can advance against a troop."
2 Samuel 22:30

My friend had a burning question. "How do I pray? Can I ask God for what I want and need, or do I stick with praying the way I learned as a child, with praise, thanksgiving and an amen? I don't want to offend God or make Him mad, and I don't want to do it wrong."

I remember asking the same question before deciding to take God at His word, "Call on me and I will answer you."[1] My spiritual life increased as I began talking with God as I would my closest friend, sitting next to me, listening to my heart and understanding the emotions behind every word. I found comfort in talking to Him aloud, not so He could hear me, but so I could know whether my words were prayers or just private thoughts.

Sincere prayer increased my awareness of God's activity and helped me recognize His answers. No longer did I see things as coincidence. Rather, I saw them as divine intervention, as God's way of responding. My world broadened as I saw God's activity in everyday life.

Our prayers, when spoken from our innermost depth, stir the heart of God.[2] He knows who we are, where we are, what we are thinking, and how we feel. God knows what we need, even before we ask. However, even though He knows us from the inside out, He will not break through a boundary we have set to keep Him at a distance. He waits to be invited into our circumstances. Our prayers welcome Him into our life, and He answers our call for companionship, guidance, help, comfort, and healing.[3]

Through earnest prayer, our spirit enables us to recognize God's activity and promptings. We listen with our senses; with sight and sound, taste and smell, touch and awareness. The more of ourselves we devote to prayer, the more our senses are stimulated to know and recognize His presence. The measurement of earnest prayer is not the amount of time spent communing with God; rather, it is humility of heart, the willingness to yield emotions and selfishness, to confess wrongs, and to listen for His response.

Prayer is vital in developing a relationship with our Creator. It opens the way for us to know God. The more we know Him, the more our prayers reflect His heart in our circumstances. The more we know Him, the better we know ourselves. It all begins with prayer. Prayer is the way forward. Step by step. Day by day.

Why a forty-day journey? Jesus willingly went into the wilderness for forty days to prepare for His ministry on Earth.[4] Let us willingly set aside forty days of growth to prepare us for our future. At the end of this forty-day journey, we will see ourselves and God through fresh eyes. We will experience spiritual growth and transformation as we lean into God and trust Him with our innermost thoughts. Welcome to day one of your forty-day journey.

PRAYER

Lord,

In my forty days of prayer, may You be my vision. Take me from self-centered to God-centered living. Teach me to follow Your ways. Help me see You through fresh eyes. Lead me to know You for who You are rather than a false belief established over the years. Open my understanding, increase my faith, and restore my vision. Burn away the desire within me to please Man. Instill a desire to please You alone. Increase my understanding of who You are. Amen.

SCRIPTURE FOR DEEPER INSIGHT

[1] Jeremiah 33:3
[2] John 11:35
[3] Isaiah 42:16
[4] Matthew 4:1-11

REFLECTIONS

What results do you hope to see at the end of this forty-day journey? (Example: Be able to more clearly hear God's voice, pray daily for my family, a greater awareness of God's presence.)

Does the thought of praying and connecting with God create anxiety or fear? Write a prayer, asking God to give you peace as you walk through this journey. If you are afraid, filled with disbelief, or worried about what this forty days may entail, journal those thoughts and emotions. This is a great first step in clearing the mind of distractions.

Day Two

UNQUENCHABLE THIRST

"I thirst." John 19:28

W hen Jesus saw Andrew and John following him, He asked, "What do you want?"[1] They wanted to know "The Lamb of God, who takes away the sin of the world!"[2] Their souls were thirsty, and they longed for a drink of spiritual water. How poetic that sounds, yet how practical to our spiritual life. Just as our physical body needs water to function properly and survive, our spiritual life needs water for the same reasons. Jesus promised, "Whoever believes in me, streams of living water will flow from within him."[3]

What is this living water? It is the indwelling presence of the Holy Spirit. When we invite Jesus into our hearts, He places within us His Spirit. He calls it a "deposit, guaranteeing what is to come,"[4] reminding us we have the promise of eternal life with God. This "deposit" increases as we yield our lives to Him and allow Him to lead, comfort, teach and guide us. As we allow, His Spirit brings about healing and change in our innermost being, transforming us into the person we are created to be. As we grow and mature in our spiritual life, the likeness of Christ overflows through us and is reflected to the outside world.

Jesus said, "Whoever drinks the water I give him will never thirst."[5] This is a promise of spiritual refreshing, available to everyone. The first step is to come to Jesus. The second is to accept His extended offer, "Come Lord Jesus. I am thirsty. You are the living water I crave. Remove the sin in my heart and fill my emptiness with Your Spirit." Jesus answers, "Come, all who are thirsty. Come to the waters that your soul may live."[6]

Just like us, Jesus experienced physical and spiritual thirst. He took on our sin while hanging on the cross. He knew the moment the sins of the world were laid on Him, because the Spirit of God departed from

Him. This is the only time Jesus experienced separation from the Father. In His agony, Jesus said, "I thirst." His unspoken meaning was, "Father, I thirst for Your presence. I thirst for the living water that connects Your Spirit with Mine." Man's answer to the thirst of Jesus was to give Him wine vinegar to satisfy His flesh. What Jesus desired was the living water of God's presence.

This message stirs my fickle heart. When I am thirsty for God, I often feed my flesh instead of my spirit. Over and again, I rediscover how sinful living produces dry springs, and my spiritual life dehydrates. My spirit cries out for living water and I give it vinegar. Water hydrates while vinegar dehydrates. Feeding my spirit reduces my craving for foods of the flesh. Feeding my flesh reduces my craving for spiritual food. Each decision feeds one or the other. With one choice, my spiritual life increases. With the other, my spiritual life decreases. The choice is mine. Living water or vinegar?

God's Word and presence are the healing prescription for our spiritual dehydration. Both cleanse, fill, establish, mature and renew us. Once we see our need for God and find nourishment in Christ, our spiritual appetite increases, and we mature.[7]

PRAYER

Father,

I long for Your presence, to saturate in Your wisdom and truth. As I share my worries and anxieties, You give peace and assurance, reminding me that You are working behind the scenes to bring about good. May I be intentional in setting aside time daily to meet with You, so my life is a fresh reflection of You rather than a stale impression. Amen.

SCRIPTURE FOR DEEPER INSIGHT

[1] John 1:29-39
[2] John 1:29
[3] John 7:38
[4] 2 Corinthians 5:5

[5] John 4:13
[6] Isaiah 55:1,3
[7] 1 Peter 2:2

REFLECTIONS

Are you spiritually dehydrated? How do you quench your spiritual thirst? With vinegar for the flesh or living water for the spirit? (Examples of vinegar for the flesh: adultery, gossip, criticism, pride, selfishness. Examples of living water for the spirit: talking with God, yielding to His ways, caring for your mind, body and spirit in ways honoring to God.)

Read Isaiah 55:1-3. Jesus says, "Come to the water and drink." What does this scripture tell you about satisfying your soul?

Day Three

MY HEART, HIS DWELLING PLACE

"How lovely is your dwelling place,
O Lord Almighty." Psalm 84:1

When I received Christ as a young girl, it was as simple as accepting His invitation of forgiveness and eternal life. As I mature, I am more aware how important that decision was and the blessing of having God's spirit within me. Scripture assures, when we become believers, our body becomes the temple for the Holy Spirit,[1] and our heart becomes His dwelling place. He lives within our inner person, and serves as teacher, guide, comforter, and so much more. His Spirit turns our internal valleys of trouble into mountains of praise. But His work is hindered unless we give Him access to the cobwebs hidden within our heart, His dwelling place.

We are cautioned to guard our heart,[2] to keep our eyes, ears and thoughts pure[3] so we don't entertain evil that will consume or overtake us. We are encouraged to follow the ways of God rather than the desires of our heart, for the heart is deceitful[4] and leads us astray.

As we venture in becoming more like Christ, the enemy prowls, looking for an opportunity to throw us off course. We are wise to stand guard over our emotions, lusts and motives so we aren't ensnared and cast into a pit of despair or a cage of entrapment.

Below are a few housekeeping items to work through. Sit with each of these, meditate on them, and see if these have taken up residence within the cobwebs of your heart. Do this heart check annually to assure you have not fallen into a trap of walking through the motions rather than living in God's way. "Father, guide my thoughts and convict me in areas where growth is needed. Amen."

- I am angry with God when things don't go well.
- I have the attitude, "God owes me because I am a good person and deserve better."
- I feel that I have the right to manipulate God to give me what I desire because I am better than most people.
- My life is rooted in myself rather than an identity in Christ.
- My prayers seek God for what He can give rather than who He is.
- I withhold forgiveness from others who have hurt me.
- I am merciless in condemning and criticizing others.
- My response to criticism is to fight back with critical arguments or defensiveness.
- I view criticism as truth and allow it to crush my spirit because my identify is in what others say rather than in who I am in Christ.
- My faith is a set of rules and manmade doctrines rather that based on the grace and truth of God and being in relationship with Him.
- My motive in serving is to elevate Self rather than serving God and discipling others.
- I believe as long as my outer life looks good to others, I don't need to do the inside work of knowing God and walking in His ways. In my life, Christianity is more of a showcase than a life change.

PRAYER

Pray the blessing below over yourself and others. Replace the words "me," "my," and "I" with the name of the one you are blessing.

Father,

Strengthen me in my inner being, so Christ may dwell in my heart through faith. Cleanse me from unhealthy habits and attitudes. Open my eyes to see my blind spots. Reveal areas in my life needing renewal and help me have the humility and the desire to surrender those areas to You, so I may learn to walk in Your ways. May I grasp the depth of Your love.[5] Amen.

SCRIPTURE FOR DEEPER INSIGHT

[1] 1 Corinthians 6:19-20
[2] Proverbs 4:23
[3] Psalm 119:9-16
[4] Jeremiah 17:9
[5] Ephesians 3:14-19

REFLECTIONS

Underline any of the items in the above list that cause a stir or conviction in your spirit. These are areas of growth to submit to the Holy Spirit for cleansing and renewal. Journal any thoughts or fears about working through these items.

Take inventory of your words, attitudes and motives. Read Matthew 12:34. What does this say about the condition of your heart?

Day Four

THE CYCLE OF SIN

*"He has sent me to proclaim freedom
to the captives."* Luke 4:18

S in touches every life. It has a hold on humanity. It is the responsibility of each person to wrestle with sin and overcome temptation. To continually yield to sin is to become enslaved. "For a man is a slave to whatever has mastered him."[1] Not only do we enslave ourselves when we walk in sin, we impact the lives of those around us. Like whirling in a tornado of life, we spin out of control, following the road of temptation wherever it leads. When we escape the twisting funnel, we fall to the ground, seeking God's forgiveness and committing to do better. Perhaps we live in freedom for a season. But if we do not master sin, the funnel of temptation returns, pulling us into its vortex, moving from place to place once again, stronger than ever.

The vortex of our sin addiction often becomes so strong we pull others along with us. "This is the life! Join me in this pleasure." Our out-of-control spinning pulls others into the depth of our unrest. As much as we laud it as being enjoyable and fun, at the end of the day, we sit alone in our shame and remorse, pleading with God to rescue us, yet again, and release us from the sin cycle. How do I know of this vortex? Years ago, I stepped into a sinful lifestyle. I was aware of my choices, yet selfishness pushed me forward, wanting my way over God's way. I tempted others to join me in the vortex, to spin out of control and wreak damage to their inner being, to follow me down a road separating them from God.

That rebellious season changed my future and created a history that stirs emotions of shame. The past is what it is; I cannot change it. But I can learn from it, taking time to consider the damage done to Self and others, processing the mistakes and the attraction that pulled me into wrong decisions, and yielding those things to God for His forgiveness and cleansing.

Until the vortex is shut down, until the temptation is yielded to God and overcome by Man, it continues to beckon, "Come back to the life of pleasure, just one more time. This time you are older and can control it." Over and over, the sinful nature leads us back into the trap of lustful pleasures, whose companions are guilt, shame, entrapment, regret and hunger for more.

The companion of peace comes only when one refuses to step back into the vortex, yielding control to God. Sin is always crouching at the door of the weak-willed, waiting for the opportunity to pounce and pull us back in.[2]

We have the rescue remedy, which is to have the mind of Christ.[3] Sin takes our mind away from God. When we allow God in, He teaches us the way of peace, freedom, and shutting the door to sin. He walks us through the process of overcoming temptation! Reclaim your best life. Take back the keys, unlock the door to freedom and evict sin and its condemning companions. Guard your mind, walk away from sin, and live in victory.

PRAYER

Father,

Thank You for the freedom I have in You, freedom from the grip of sin, from guilt, shame, and condemnation. Give me strength to continue to walk away from sin, surrendering my natural lusts to You and striving for a pure heart. May pride and rebellion be cast off and replaced with a desire to know You.

Soften the heart of my unbelieving family and friends and open their eyes to Your goodness. Place godly people in their path daily to plant seeds of love, peace, forgiveness and freedom. I know Your desire is for all to come to You and for none to perish. Hold me faithful in praying for them, for Your love to be known and received, and for eternal life to be their greatest gift. Amen.

SCRIPTURE FOR DEEPER INSIGHT

[1] 2 Peter 2:18
[2] Genesis 4:7
[3] Romans 8

REFLECTIONS

We all struggle. Are there areas of sin in your life you struggle to release?

How can you take first steps to be an overcomer in this area? Where would you like to see this area in your life changed during this forty-day journey? Remember these three words. "Help me, Lord." Use them often!

Consider talking with a trusted friend about this area of sin, asking them to pray for your strength and courage to be free from this area. Remember to show grace to yourself in the areas you struggle. Life is a journey, walked step by step, day by day.

Day Five

·•◆•◆•◆•◆•·

GRACE AND GRUMBLING

"Trust in the Lord with all your heart and lean not on your own understanding." Proverbs 3:5

I was co-leading a college ministry and it was deemed we needed a newsletter for communicating with the students. With a degree in administration and a background in marketing, the task was delegated to me. I gathered stories, articles, and event dates; I designed and edited the newsletter, then I sent it to the students. I was a one-man show, not seeking input from teammates or my co-leader. I was determined to show everyone what I could do. (The "I" count in the preceding paragraph equals seven.)

After distributing the newsletter, my co-leader called with several suggestions, corrections, and rewrites. I was livid. "I did exactly what you asked. Who are you to criticize? If you wanted control, you should have done it yourself!" My pride and ego were bruised. As I raised my voice in defensiveness, I expected her to respond likewise. Instead, she listened to my outburst, apologized, and ended the call.[1] Minutes later, she phoned back. "Great," I thought, "Now I will gain the satisfaction of having a screaming match." Wrong.

Her tone was gentle as she spoke. "You are right. You did exactly what was asked, and you did a great job. The students will be blessed. My perfectionism kicked in and the edits suggested are not only unnecessary but would make the newsletter too corporate. Thank you for your hard work. I hope you can forgive me."

I was speechless. How could she show such undeserved kindness? She knew something in her Christian walk I had yet to learn. Leaning into Christ and displaying His character, despite a verbal attack, silences an argument and produces a sense of shame and humility in the heart of the refuter. Scripture says, "If your enemy is hungry, feed him; if he is thirsty, give him something to drink. In doing this, you will heap burning coals on his head."[2] In other words, be kind to people who yell at you, and your kindness will put them to shame.

Her gracious response to my grumbling complaint crashed the wall of pride I attempted to erect between our relationship. Humility opened my eyes to a hidden truth. My motive in being a ministry co-leader was more for elevating myself than discipling the students. What were my motives? To prove I was a leader, showcase my administrative and marketing skills, and gain the praise of others who recognized my success in building a ministry from scratch.

Hear this truth. When motive behind ministry is for personal and selfish gain, the fruitfulness of the work will be greatly limited. God sees our heart, He knows our motives, and He will not spiritually bless or sustain activities done in His name when the motive is self-interest and the glory is used for self-elevation. His ways are not our ways. Let us lean into Him for understanding; let us trust Him to direct our path. Let us consistently check our motives and, as often as necessary, realign them with the passion and purpose God has called us to rather than selfish gain. This is the way forward.

PRAYER

Father,

Thank You for Your Word that guides my life and prompts me in right living. Help me stand firm in Your truth and not fall into the temptation to use Your name for self-elevation. Help me not compromise my faith or behavior for anyone or any reason. May I humbly walk in truth, showing grace and compassion toward others, without judgment, while standing strong on the foundation of my faith and belief. May my life reflect You in every way. Forgive me for following others in ways that compromise my faith and forgive me for encouraging others to follow me into compromising their convictions. Help me remove the rebellion rooted so deeply in my nature. Amen.

SCRIPTURE FOR DEEPER INSIGHT

[1] Proverbs 15:1
[2] Romans 12:20

REFLECTIONS

Has anyone extended to you an overwhelming gift of grace? How did their actions influence your understanding of mature Christian characteristics?

Have you extended unexpected grace to someone? If so, what was the outcome?

Take a moment to evaluate your motives in serving others. Is it for selfish gain and recognition, or do you serve out of love for God and His children?

Day Six

·•◆◆◆•·

THE SILENT UNDERTOW

*"Your commands make me wiser than my enemies,
for they are ever with me."* Psalm 119:98

We lived in a nice house in a friendly neighborhood, there was food on the table and clothes on our backs. We had friends and a church family. The four children were healthy and involved in various activities. There were a few challenges with parent/child relationships, but nothing that raised the decibel level in the house. We were a strong family. With one exception. There was a silent undertow pulling me in a direction I didn't notice until hindsight hit me with regret.

At some point, the responsibilities of caring for a home, family, full-time job, and volunteer activities became overwhelming and moved me into auto-pilot-mom-mode, struggling to keep up with the demands. The harder I worked, the quieter I became. Most conversations centered around "to-do" lists, "Do your homework. Take a shower. Make your bed. Walk the dog." Other conversations were check lists. "Did you clean the bathroom? Have you swept the kitchen?" I had a great love and affection for my family, and I tried to stay engaged, but it was difficult. Outspoken words were unintentionally limited; I was exhausted and talking was another task requiring thought and energy, so I didn't talk. But listening was easy. So, I listened to the children talk about their day as they followed me around the house. All the while, the silent undertow continued to pull.

Relationships are not built nor sustained when the to-do list, check-list, or one-way conversations are the focus of discussion. Humans seek unconditional love and the need to be understood and appreciated. The spoken word is invaluable in conveying emotion.[1] Love can be shown when actions and words come into alignment, but hear this, children and spouses need affirming words saying, "I'm proud of you," "Tell me about your day," "I am thankful for you."[2] When two-way conversations are limited, there are broken connections, and loneliness has a way of creeping in. If left unchecked, loneliness can act out in negative attitudes and behaviors such as depression, anger, criticism, or in my case, the silent undertow of discontentment.

A friend recognized the shift and suggested I start a thank-you journal to change my perspective from lack to gratitude. After a few weeks, my daughter read the journal and said, "I'm surprised I'm mentioned in your book." My heart sank. How could she be surprised? I was reminded of a time my other daughter expressed, "Mom, I never hear you talk." I hadn't taken her words to heart at the time, but now they stung. In my distraction and busyness, I failed to nurture my family with words. "Lord, open my lips and release the power of this undertow."

The thank-you journal served a dual purpose. It reminded me of the importance of gratitude, and revealed the treasures contained in the spoken word. Today my heart celebrates as I have fresh opportunities to visit with my adult children and grandchildren, listening intently, asking questions, and enjoying intimacy without to-do lists. Regrets become life lessons when we submit them to God.

PRAYER

Father,

Help me slow down so I have time and energy to focus on relationships with You and others. May I use the spoken word to teach, encourage, affirm, correct, and comfort, seasoned with love, grace, and kindness. Make me aware of any negative or critical tones in my expressions and actions, that I may grow in these areas. May I remember to give You thanks for all situations and circumstances, knowing You work all things out for my best and Your glory. May my thanksgiving overflow into the hearts and lives of my family. Amen.

SCRIPTURE FOR DEEPER INSIGHT

[1] Proverbs 16:24
[2] 1 Thessalonians 5:11
[3] Psalm 103:15

REFLECTIONS

Consider keeping a thank-you journal for the remainder of this forty-day journey. Watch your attitude shift to one of gratitude.

Do the activities in your schedule take away from your opportunity to have meaningful conversations with your family? If so, how can you remedy the situation, so your hindsight vision does not cause you to grieve missed opportunities?

Let us be faithful in carrying forward words of encouragement and thanksgiving, beginning with those closest to us. Our days are like grass.[3] Let us be like the refreshing dew watering the souls of others with spoken words of purpose and affirmation. May they know daily we are thankful for them as we lift them in prayer to our Eternal Father.

Day Seven

CONVERSATION PEACE

"A man of knowledge uses words with restraint." Proverbs 17:27

As a dinner guest, I sat across from the parents, watching them engage in an impromptu conversation with their daughter, soon to be eighteen and out of high school. Her post-graduation plans were less than desirable, as they involved too much freedom with minimal boundaries or structure. I didn't know how to gracefully excuse myself, so I observed in silence.

Communication was often strained, as each party searched for words to express their point of view, but voices were not raised, tempers did not flare, and opinions were spoken without righteous or accusing tones. No one left the table in tears or threw tantrums when their thoughts were not met with approval. An adult conversational style was displayed, each person respectful of the other, listening without interruption, and not pressuring the others to agree. Clearly, these mature patterns had been modeled in the marriage and used in the upbringing of their children.

A few days after this exchange, I had an opportunity to practice what I observed. When the conversation took a controversial turn, I remembered to listen with my ears and engage my heart. Where defensiveness might have taken the front seat before, now it was locked away in a trunk with other immature practices. After all, defensiveness escalates arguments, and I wanted to understand the depth of what was communicated. Emotions are often difficult to convey, and when we don't stop to listen with heart and head, we misunderstand the main point. Without understanding, self-interest is quick to rise and limit conversations, staging our opinions, advice, or staunch views as the best way forward. When we listen, engage, and ask questions from a heart of concern rather than a point of judgment or bias, we move forward in unity, regardless of the outcome.

Though I knew of this style and maturity of communication, I had not experienced it first-hand. Putting this method into practice broadened me in unexpected yet rewarding ways! Since I doubt this family will demonstrate their dinner time conversations with the world, included below are helpful communication tips from scripture:

- Everyone should be quick to listen, slow to speak and slow to become angry.[1]
- A hot-tempered person stirs dissension, but a patient person calms a quarrel.[2]
- He who answers before listening – that is his folly and his shame.[3]
- Love is patient, love is kind. It does not boast, it is not rude, it is not self-seeking, it is not easily angered, it keeps no record of wrongs.[4]
- A gentle answer turns away wrath, but a harsh word stirs anger.[5]
- Fathers do not embitter your children, or they will become discouraged.[6]
- Speaking the truth in love, we will in all things mature in Christ.[7]

PRAYER

Father,

Strengthen our family. May we have grace, forgiveness and unconditional love toward one another. Strengthen our communication skills that are foundational to our marriage and family. May our vows of commitment stand the tests of time as we lean into problem-solving together, seeking and trusting You to give wisdom. May we seek unity rather than self-centered gain. Bind our love with Your threefold cord. Lord, through better or worse, through richer or poorer, may our hearts beat as one, strong and steady! May we always be committed to weather out the storms of life together. May our family, throughout all generations, value marriage, commitment, communication, and unity. Hold us steady in You. Amen.

SCRIPTURE FOR DEEPER INSIGHT

[1] James 1:19
[2] Proverbs 15:18
[3] Proverbs 18:13
[4] 1 Corinthians 13:4-6
[5] Proverbs 15:1
[6] Colossians 3:21
[7] Ephesians 4:15

REFLECTIONS

How would you rate the communication skills of your family? Where can you incorporate more respect or grace to improve communications with one or all of your family members?

Are there Biblical principles you can put into place to create a greater balance and foundation for difficult discussions?

Day Eight

CONSIDER THE COST

*"And this is love, that we walk in obedience
to His commands."* 1 John 1:6

We begin our path of obedience by applying God's teachings in the simplest of ways. Perhaps we want to apply scripture about "being kind toward others,"[1] so we leave the closest parking spot for someone else, or we alert the cashier when we are undercharged for an item. As we grow in faith, we may apply the same scripture differently by making visits to shut-ins or donating food to a shelter. As growth continues, the same verse remains applicable, yet stretches us further, perhaps in relocating to teach the Gospel or volunteering at a site devastated by a hurricane.

As we grow closer to God, we surrender to follow Him in all things, asking Him to mold our heart of rebellion into a heart of obedience. With this new heart, we learn to draw near to God, to walk in His ways, and to leave the results to Him. We are encouraged to steer our hearts toward God because we love Him and desire to represent His love to others. Yet, we are also instructed to consider the cost of following Christ, so we understand our commitment.

This walk of obedience was modeled by Christ, as was the hardship of walking this narrow road, and misunderstood by natural man. Just as the apostles were tempted and tested to see if they would fall away when times grew tough, our devotion to Christ is tested when we face decisions, hardship, ridicule, rejection, selfishness and betrayal. Will we falter under the attempts of the enemy to destroy us or will we stand strong in our faith?

Years ago, I awakened with a burning question on my mind. "Whom shall I send? Who will go?"[2] I knew the question was from God, and I cautiously considered the answer. Was I willing to go wherever God sent?

Eventually, I gave my response, "Send me, Lord." Months later, our family was relocated to a new state. Each time the Lord presented this question, my answer was the same. Moving from state to state meant leaving family and friends. The heartbreak was real, the burden was heavy. Yet I knew in following Christ wholeheartedly, sacrifices were required. Through answering His call, He increased my family, faith, ministry, and friends one-hundred-fold and brought me to a place of wholeness and purpose. The walk of faith stretches, pushes, and matures us, growing us into the likeness of Christ, and telling the world we are His. The blessings of obedience far outweigh the cost of discipleship!

As followers of Christ, we will be placed in the refiner's fire[3] of testing for purging and shaping our character into a glorious display of His splendor. Many times, the tool used to complete the work is one of great cost. Will we prevail and come through the testing fires as refined gold? Will our love and devotion to Christ sustain the heat of life's battles? A heart of obedience considers the cost and responds, "Send me, Lord."

PRAYER

Father,

Give me a heart of obedience to love others and walk in Your ways. May I seek to become more like You by giving priority to Your Word and applying Your teachings. Give me understanding in how to break scripture into bite-size pieces for daily application. When the trials of life come, may I be found faithful in believing Your promises, walking in Your ways, and submitting to Your plan so my character may be refined as pure gold. Amen.

SCRIPTURE FOR DEEPER INSIGHT

[1] Ephesians 4:32
[2] Isaiah 6:8
[3] Malachi 3:3
[4] Judges 6:36-40

REFLECTIONS

How have you experienced joy and suffering in being a follower of Christ?

How do you balance the knowledge of joy and suffering that accompany living a life of faith?

Oftentimes, we become stuck in our spiritual growth because we refuse to take a step of faith in obedience. What step of obedience has God placed before you where faith and fear collide? Ask God to give you courage to take this step of obedience. If you are confused whether it is God's leading, ask Him to give you confirmation that this direction is from Him.[4]

Day Nine

EMOTIONS AND GRIEF

"Come to me, all who are weary and burdened,
and I will give you rest." Matthew 11:28

In His Sovereignty, the Lord knew I needed to grieve old hurts and loss because a new grief was on the horizon that would take every ounce of strength to walk through. He orchestrated a way for this to happen at a Dragonfly Ministries retreat. Though I was the retreat leader, my emotions struggled to engage, as I knew once the emotional dam was breached, the floodwaters would burst. Our family was in the process of relocating to another state, putting great distance between us and our Texas daughters. My emotions were tied in knots as I pushed back the grief and depression of the move and fought against other hidden hurts pressing to escape the depth of my spirit.

When the retreat members headed into a time of solitude, I sat alone, numb, thankful for the silence. A young woman approached and said, "I am a grief counselor, and I sense sadness in you. I believe I am here to help you work through past loss." The "retreat leader" in me wanted to tell her to stop talking and go into her time of silence, but my "hurt little girl" wanted to crawl into her lap and cry. The "hurt little girl" won.

She asked questions drawing me into the discovery of buried wounds. The questions revealed areas of life covered beneath a layer of fear. I was afraid to admit guilt or take accountability for anything I may have done to cause the hurts. To protect Self, I habitually ignored my emotions of sadness and grief. In refusing to process the hurts, however, I bottled the grief in a canister ready to explode. Things like a miscarriage, the divorce of my parents, my father's illness, and the relocation to another state. Would my daughters forgive me for moving away? As each wound was resurrected, I was encouraged to grieve the pain. This woman's help was difficult to accept, and her suggestions were even harder. I did not want anyone to see me cry, yet something within knew the way forward was to release the burden to Jesus so He could provide healing. God gave me a treasure through this woman's obedience. He set me free from constipating grief as the release came through my tears.

Grieving is hard work. It involves facing pain we prefer to bury or to numb. Many times, grief only requires processing thoughts, then allowing anger or sadness to escape the inward prison of our psyche. Other times, grief involves taking ownership of mistakes we have made. We endure a process of seeing Self through honest eyes, grieving the pain we have brought upon Self and others; pain we have pushed away, unwilling to reconcile until a later time. Grief is not our enemy; rather, it purges us of emotions that, if held within, build a wall around our heart and prevent us from abundant living. Be encouraged – as grief is processed, the pain once hidden is released to Jesus, who replaces it with peace and healing. Do the work and experience His rest. He is acquainted with grief. He is a "Man of Sorrows."[1] He is our Comforter[2] and desires to trade our pain for His peace.

PRAYER

Father,

Touch me and make me whole. Heal my emotions – those feelings hidden deep within because the pain is too great. Give me the strength to look within and do the inner work of feeling the pain of past brokenness. Give me the courage to allow the pain to be resurrected and grieved so I may be healed and restored to the person You created me to be. I am weary of running. Help me face and work through the inner wounds, realizing my wholeness and healing will be a light to others who struggle with similar hurts. I desire to be my best for You and for those You put in my pathway. Infuse me with Your courage and strength. Amen.

SCRIPTURE FOR DEEPER INSIGHT

[1] Isaiah 53:3
[2] John 14:16-17

REFLECTIONS

Have you hidden or buried sadness and loss you need to grieve and release so you can again experience life's abundance?

What holds you back from processing through past hurts and failures? Fear of Self? Fear of acceptance? Ask God to give you courage to do a thorough self-evaluation so the work of healing can complete in your life.

Day Ten

PEW TRIPPING

"If you hold anything against anyone,
forgive them." Mark 11:25b

The last thing I wanted to do was apologize. After all, I wasn't the one who sent the condemning emails. Her slanderous words threatened to damage my reputation, and her unjustified anger attempted to beat me into the ground like a tent peg. What was her trigger? She had a history of relationship issues. Why was I involved? My vulnerability in sharing personal insecurities put a target on my heart, and the enemy's shot hit the mark.

Accusations were taken to God to see if there was truth in what my accuser said. Counsel was sought from ministry partners and friends to glean wisdom and reveal blind spots within my character. The enemy was on the prowl, so I prayed for protection and maturity to shake off the thoughts of counter-attack. However, faith and stillness were not my state of mind. I needed to be justified and cleared, so I rehearsed her words in my mind, allowing them to sting my ego over and over. Eventually, the seed of bitterness germinated in my heart and threatened to take root.

One Sunday in church, I sat on the front pew, as far from my accuser as possible. She was tucked away in a back pew, on the opposite side of the church. "Good," I thought. "She will be out the door before I am forced to acknowledge her presence." God's thoughts, however, were to the contrary, and His plan was to administer healing by root plucking.

As we stood to sing the final song, the Holy Spirit prompted me. You know the feeling. You are minding your business, when suddenly, your heartrate increases, a random thought enters your mind, and you know without doubt God is giving direction. He prompted me to walk to the back of the church and seek forgiveness from my accuser. I questioned,

"In front of all these people? I'm on the front pew! Besides, I didn't start this argument, why should I apologize?" My heart rate increased. I had a choice – obey or ignore (also known as disobedience).

Mid-song, I stepped into the center aisle and moved toward her. She saw me coming. As I scooted into her pew, she stiffened. My course was set and, from this point, clumsily executed. I tripped over feet and knocked a hymnal out of someone's hand. Why are pews so long and closely situated? Alas, I stood by her side. I looked into her eyes, expecting to see hatred or bitterness. Rather, her eyes revealed pain from a trail of rejection. In an instant, I was aware of a truth that eluded me for days. An innocent action on my part was incorrectly interpreted on her part, triggering an emotional wound. Her survival instinct was to shoot before being shot. Without words, I understood her pain and was filled with compassion. I whispered, "I'm sorry. Will you forgive me?" She answered, "Yes." God's ways bring healing.

Don't miss the message here. Too often, we harbor hurts and misunderstandings never intended in the way interpreted. Barriers block relationships because incorrect assumptions are made. As Christ-followers, we are to take the first step in rectifying broken relationships so unforgiveness and bitterness do not take root in our heart and grow into trees of unfruitfulness.

PRAYER

Father,

Reveal to me bitterness, resentment, or fears holding me hostage to broken relationships. Give me courage to walk in Your ways and to do the uncomfortable things to bring forgiveness. Help me peel away the layers and discover what is nestled deep within and interferes with my relationships, thoughts and passions. Bring freedom, that I may love without expectation and fear, serve you without hesitation and distance, and be Your messenger of healing. May any unforgiveness or negativity I hold be revealed. Amen.

SCRIPTURE FOR DEEPER INSIGHT

Isaiah 55:8-9
Matthew 6:14-15
[1] Quote by Marianne Williamson

REFLECTIONS

Does this quote by Marianne Williamson resonate with you? If so, how?

> *"Unforgiveness is like drinking poison yourself and waiting for the other person to die."* [1]

Have you taken on a battle to defend yourself, knowing God wanted to use kindness and love as His teaching tools rather than your own justification and defensiveness?

Read Galatians 5:22-23. What are the fruits of the Spirit? If living by the Spirit, how do you display Christ-like characteristics in situations where you are tempted to use justification and defensiveness to clear your name?

Day Eleven

REFINER'S FIRE

*"He will purify and refine them like
gold and silver."* Malachi 3:3

Something was missing within; an emptiness that beckoned, "There is more in life." A second voice chided, "Your 'good girl' image has robbed you of happiness." I believed the second voice, the lie, because Satan repeated what I had been told in my teenage years. Same lie, different season of life; both times the lie trumped God's truth because it was easier to believe I am not-enough than to find identity in the unconditional love and acceptance of Christ. Rather than leaning into God to discover the purpose and depth of my emptiness, I opened the door to sin, which wooed me over the threshold from light into the darkness.[1] It only took one step, one decision, to transform my heart for God into a heart of stone, hardened by rebellion, selfishness, sin, and pride. I shook off conviction and took another step into darkness, through another decision, and a barrier was placed between me and my intimate relationship with Christ. Why? Because I allowed sin to rob me of my innocence, pulling me into the shadow of forbidden lust.*

What was I searching for in this dark detour? Unconditional love and abiding presence.[2] What did I find? Heaviness of heart, guilt, shallow affection, disappointment, and a bottomless pit of discontent. My path was far from the One who held the answer to my emptiness. When this lifestyle lost its attraction, I turned back toward the light of Christ. He met me as I called out and gave me unconditional love and forgiveness. He returned me to the light. He never left me.

Stepping back into His light revealed the damage done to my heart when I walked in sin. This damage had to be healed and purified. He placed me in the refiner's fire.[3] The heat from the flames was often unbearable, as

I saw myself for who I truly was. He revealed the depth of sin within that justified the journey into darkness. In His gentle way, He uncovered wrong patterns, beliefs, and selfish ideas that fed into my decision to betray Him and follow my own desires. Little by little, He showed me the person I was beneath the outer façade. The stinging of truth humbled me and sent me to my knees, seeking the better way, the way of truth. Since I walked away from Christ, I understood the pain of life without Him. This wisdom caused me to press into God and allow Him to do the painful refining work instead of running away again. He transformed my heart of stone back into a heart of flesh.[4] The ashes of my sin and hardened heart were placed in the pouring of my new foundation in Christ. I will never again retreat, for my feet are set upon the rock of my salvation, Jesus Christ.

We cannot heal ourselves, we cannot go into the depth of our own life and uncover the cobwebs without God's guidance and healing hand. To grow is to endure the pain and truth of who we have become, to surrender those areas to God, and to yield to Him for complete healing. It's hard work that takes courage, humility, and time. It is the way forward to abundant life.

PRAYER

Father,

Forgive my wayward lifestyle and bring me into the light of Your presence. Give me courage to look at my inner life, to see the damage done by submitting to selfish desires and caving to the lies of Satan instead of Your truth. I desire to live for You, from the inside out. Walk me through the process of recognizing sinful patterns and yielding them to You for renewal. Amen.

SCRIPTURE FOR DEEPER INSIGHT

[1] Genesis 4:7
[2] Hebrews 13:5
[3] Malachi 3:3
[4] Ezekiel 36:26

*You can read my story in *The Making of a Dragonfly, Following Christ Through the Winds of Change.*

REFLECTIONS

When you are ready, seek God's forgiveness for lifestyle choices that have, now or in the past, put a barrier between you and God.

Spiritual growth takes place from the inside of our being. God shines a light in our heart, revealing motives, attitudes, and self-centeredness. His ways are gentle and loving, and He wants what is best for you. Seeing the reality of the inner life is painful and humbling, but God is a faithful companion who lovingly leads from brokenness to healing, step by step. Trust Him. Take a dive into the inner you. Get a look at the driving force behind your actions, attitudes, decisions, and motives. What do you see? Surrender broken areas to Christ and invite Him to infuse you with truth and healing.

Day Twelve

RETURN TO ME

*"Return to me, for I am gracious, compassionate,
slow to anger, abounding in love."* Joel 2:13

As I prepared for a job interview, my thoughts raced to consider the timing for stepping into a new career. Was I ready to go from the corporate world to a nonprofit organization? Was I ready to take on the responsibility of spiritual leadership? I opened my Bible in search of answers. "You have made known to me the path of life."[1] I closed my eyes and heard His voice, as He whispered, "My child, this is the path I have chosen for you. In this role, you will be my voice." Thankful for His answer, I placed the interview and opportunity in His hands.

My new role within the nonprofit was to recruit, train, and encourage volunteers in the work of evangelism within their communities, traveling from the northernmost tip of Wisconsin to the southernmost tip of Illinois. At each stop, I was to deliver an inspirational message. Not knowing the women or their needs, I inquired of the Lord for His words, incorrectly assuming it would be the same for each location.

Before one such event, as I was looking over my notes, I sensed a prompting from the Lord, directing me to a different passage. He spoke, "Return to me." "Oh Lord, are You changing the message at the last minute? How can I speak these words to Christian women? Their ministry is evangelism!" His words flooded my thoughts and I penned them as He spoke. I was to encourage the volunteers to walk in obedience and faith, reminding them their service was to the Lord, not to impress Man, build a bigger ministry, or elevate Self to a higher leadership position. They were not to allow prestige or status to interfere with His work. They were to return to serving Him, not the nonprofit or Self. This was God's message and I was to be the mouthpiece and deliverer of His word. I had my marching orders. Fleeing came to mind, but obedience pushed me forward.

I arrived at the venue and, when cued, shared His heart. The room was uncomfortably silent as I returned to my seat, awaiting the backlash. Finally, the event chair stood and dismissed the meeting. I gathered my things, aware the Lord had released a word of correction into the atmosphere, not sure whether to run or hide. Hesitantly, women approached to say, "thank you." The next day, I received a call from corporate headquarters. They caught wind of "the word" and asked me to share at an upcoming departmental meeting. As the same message was shared with corporate staff, the room fell silent. A time of repentance followed, inviting God to return to His role as center-focus of the ministry. For the duration of my employment, God provided opportunities to stretch and test me in being His voice to His children. His fresh word kept my spirit from becoming stale.

Surely God knows the heart of His children and delivers the Word we need, at the right time. Who are we to second guess His wisdom? Perhaps "His Word" is also for you.

HIS WORD

My child, return to Me. Forget the things of the past and return to Me. I am your first love.

Remember when you came to Me, when you sought after Me with all your heart? Remember the joy of your salvation, the way you were caught off guard at My Creation, the sunrise and the s unset, the sound and promptings of My voice? Remember the way you shared your thoughts and emotions with Me, your joys and your pain? Return to Me and let Me be the desire of your heart, the happiness you seek, the One who satisfies and fills.

Set aside the work you do out of obligation and commitments made long ago, and let Me fill you with My presence, My love, a new commitment to love and seek Me. Sit and learn as I teach you personally. I am your teacher. When the greatest commandment is lived out, when you love Me first, everything else will come easily and naturally. When you make Me the desire of your heart, the priority of your life, then you will be intentional in living out your life for Me! Seek Me first! Love Me first![2]

SCRIPTURE FOR DEEPER INSIGHT

[1] Psalm 16:11
[2] Matthew 22:38

REFLECTIONS

Has God spoken a word of correction to you through someone else? How did you respond?

Has God used you to speak correction to someone? Were you able to speak it and leave the results to Him?

How does the prayer included in this devotional speak to you personally?

Day Thirteen

TROUBLE OR AFFLICTION

*"Perseverance must finish its work so that you
are mature and complete."* James 1:4

Someone asked, "Would you rather have trouble or affliction?" The obvious answer is neither, but that wasn't the question. At the shock of the one questioning, I answered, "Affliction."

Trouble will follow us all the days of our life.[1] Most times it will be a distraction, annoyance, or unexpected expense. However, for the most part, troubled circumstances are things we can fix or navigate in our own strength with our own resources. The lessons learned are generally shallow and fail to redirect life or thinking. In trouble, we may cry out to God, but the prayer is a call for the frustration to disappear, exclaiming, "Lord, rescue me from this!"

Affliction brings a rendering, a tearing of the heart. It is unbearable agony, suffering and sorrow whose cure is outside the power of Man's quick-fix. It strips away our security, leaving us grasping for understanding. Consider the story of Job. After losing his children, home, and riches, his physical health was attacked. Job was in such a state of shock and sorrow his friends did not recognize him. They "sat on the ground with him for seven days and seven nights. No one said a word to him, because they saw how great his suffering was."[2] The cry of the heart in affliction is, "Lord, deliver me through this."

We cannot move through life escaping loss and pain. Affliction produces change because it accompanies loss, whether associated with health, relationships or lifestyle. Going back to the old way of life is impossible, and we must forge a new way ahead. The choice is to accept the change and grow better or harden our heart and become bitter. Yielding to God's way produces spiritual growth and maturity; battling against God's way results in stunted growth. To yield is to release the "right to Self" inviting Him to lead. "Lord, what is Your way forward? Show me what needs to be burned away as a result of this loss and pain."

I do not ask God to bring affliction and trouble into my life. "I find it easier to obey than to suffer, to bear the cross than to hang upon it. Yet I cannot go back, for I have come too near the unseen cross, and its virtues have pierced too deeply within me."[3] Yet, in my desperation for God, I surrender all to Him, and walk through affliction and trouble with my focus on Christ, asking for the faith and courage to submit every situation to God so He can mature me into the person He created me to be. Trouble and affliction will come; it's what we do with it that matters. If you are in affliction, if you are facing gut-wrenching hardship, keep moving forward, step by step. God promises to walk with us, leading us toward a better life. When we allow, God uses the furnace of affliction[3] to our advantage. He grows us more into His likeness, He draws us near, and He redirects our path in a way that makes us a clearer representation and reflection of who we are created to be.

PRAYER

Father,

Help me endure hardship through trouble, pain and affliction with faith You are always with me, working behind the scenes, to bring about good from every situation. Help me through every battle to praise You rather than blame You, knowing each battle brings me closer to You. Though I do not always understand life's harder days, I trust You to work good from evil. Use this pain for Your glory. Heal me, Lord, not with a temporary fix, which is my way, but with eternal change. You are God, and there is no other. Amen.

SCRIPTURE FOR DEEPER INSIGHT

[1] John 16:33
[2] Job 2:7-13

[3] Cowman, Mrs. Charles E. *Streams in the Desert*. Grand Rapids: Zondervan, 1997

REFLECTIONS

Would you rather have trouble or affliction? Explain.

How have you leaned into God during times of trouble and affliction? Have you experienced shallow or deep growth in these times?

Day Fourteen

HEART AND HIP

"Honor your father and mother, that it may go well with you." Ephesians 6:2

Seeking the approval of my father, I often helped him with projects and chores. He taught me about bottle collecting, woodworking, and printing presses. I also helped Mom, but the chores she assigned were less exciting and centered around dishes, clothes, and food. When I entered a room, she put me to work, so I stayed out of her view as much as possible. As a teen, I wanted more freedom than she was willing to give, so I developed an attitude that put distance between us. It was an emotional tug-of-war to balance obedience with independence.

Moving into adulthood, the strain on our mother/daughter relationship remained. I expected her to become the Mom I thought I needed. I have since learned, when we expect people to change their personality to meet our needs, we set ourselves up for disappointment and resentment. Both emotions were buried within my heart toward Mom, as I wanted something she could not give. It took a long season to come to this realization. The disconnect in our relationship bothered me, until finally, I asked God to remove the barrier and help us reconnect. I did not know a heart-change was on the horizon. Had I known, I would have assumed the change was within Mom's heart. Au contraire. Mom's heart was never hardened toward me. However, my "little girl hurts" followed me into adulthood, and my unreasonable and unmet expectations calloused a heart that needed softening.

I sensed a prompting to invite Mom for a visit to Illinois. Summers in the South are humid, and I thought she might appreciate a break from the heat. She decided to stay two weeks; however, God had an extended stay in mind so He could do the work of softening my heart, and He did so with deep-stabbing pain. One morning, I heard a thump. When I checked on Mom, she was on the floor, unconscious. The Emergency Medical Technicians were unable to rouse her, so they transported her to the hospital. The fear of losing a mama has a way of softening a heart. The doctor said Mom had a seizure, which caused the fall, and the fall caused a broken hip. She went into surgery for hip replacement, then to a rehabilitation facility for several weeks. Soon after her hospital release, she again lost balance and fell. Though she didn't appear to be in pain, she could not move. Again, the ambulance transported her to the hospital and wheeled her into radiology. Not wanting to let her out of sight, I waited in the hospital hallway. As the staff moved Mom from the stretcher to the imaging table, she let out a gut-wrenching wail, which sent me to my knees in weakness. Her cry was the scalpel used to remove the callouses of my heart. The fall broke her other hip, so she had another round of surgery and rehabilitation. After eight months in Illinois, she returned to South Carolina. She survived two hip replacement surgeries; I survived heart surgery.

God answered my prayer. As Mom was leaving to go home, she said, "Mary, this was a hard trip, but I would not change it for the world. I got my daughter back." Enough said.

PRAYER

Father,

Create in me a pure heart. Walk me through the process, layer by layer and step by step of surrendering my selfishness, scars, and wrong thinking to You. Give me courage to look deep within to see my hardness of heart. Help me recognize the unreasonable expectations I have placed on others. Lord, instead of asking You to change them to meet my needs, I am asking You, please change me. May I lay my expectations at Your feet, knowing You alone can help me correct my thoughts, desires, and wants. Forgive me for allowing resentment and bitterness to take root and teach me to protect my heart so this does not happen again. Thank You for the gentle ways You teach and guide me, Lord. Help me lean into You in every area of life for completeness and wholeness. Amen.

SCRIPTURE FOR DEEPER INSIGHT

Psalm 51:10
Ephesians 6:1-3

REFLECTIONS

Have unmet expectations toward others caused resentment or bitterness to take root in your heart? Before answering with a quick "No," sit with this question.

Inviting God to cleanse your heart brings freedom. He reveals heart-stains layer by layer, and He walks us through the healing process step-by-step. If you are willing, take a moment to read today's prayer again, sincerely inviting Him to begin the work within you of heart cleansing. Journal the areas of growth He reveals.

Day Fifteen

GIVE ME MY MOUNTAIN

"Blessed is the man who trusts in the Lord, whose confidence is in Him." Jeremiah 17:7

The thrill of adventure had waned. Perhaps it was due to a chemical imbalance or the result of long cold winters in Illinois. I couldn't put my finger on the cause. I had an artillery of promises from God, reminding me He had a plan and purpose, but He had not given me a blueprint, timeline or roadmap to follow. I was desperate to move forward, to reclaim my sense of passion and adventure, yet it seemed I was stuck in a season of loneliness and isolation.

I searched for words to express my anguish and cried out the only thing that came to mind, "Lord, give me my mountain!" I trusted God to be my rescue, aware of His abiding presence, yet the slide continued. The way forward seemed to be downward, through the valley of storms, disappointments, and destruction. Apparently, the way to the mountaintop was through the valley of trouble.

Grasping tightly to my Shepherd, I followed Him step-by-step through the valley of the shadow of death and darkness. His footsteps lead me into the eye of the storm and my only choice was to lean into Him and stay in stride. The winds of change toppled my earthly foundation and destroyed my worldly security. Had it not been for the constant presence, comfort and protection of the Savior, the passage through the storm would have been insufferable. Still, in the valley, He restored my soul.[1] He taught me lessons that cannot be learned on the mountaintop. He increased my faith and staked my foundation in His love and sovereignty. He used the storm to prepare me for the days ahead. After a season, the sun burst through the clouds and I could see the mountain of God's promise in the distance.

It was then I remembered the story of Caleb.[2] Because of his faithfulness to God, Caleb was promised an inheritance once the Israelites entered and conquered the Promised Land. After seven years of battle, Caleb approached Joshua and said, "I am as strong today as the day Moses sent me out. Now give me this mountain the Lord promised me." Why did Caleb tell Joshua he was strong? As the Israelites cleared the land, the enemy sought refuge in Caleb's mountain. Taking possession of his promise would require additional battle.

Lightbulb moment. When I asked God to give me my mountain, I invited Him to lead me into death valley so my fears, strongholds and false beliefs could be exposed and conquered. Had I understood the meaning of the prayer, perhaps I would have relinquished my hold on God's promise to prevent the painful days that followed. Nonetheless, God used my season of loneliness and isolation to bring me to my promised destiny, filled with passion and purpose.

God's school of preparation often involves valleys, storms, and battles. Yield to Him the areas in your life needing His touch. Lean into Him and keep stride as He prepares you for days ahead.

PRAYER

Lord,

As we walk through the valleys and mountaintops of our spiritual journey, we are given opportunities to grow into Your likeness. May our focus remain on You, so we don't miss the lessons along the way. You are our Creator, the Rock on which we stand. In You, we find value, approval, acceptance, and identity. Through Your eyes, we have significance and purpose, we have Your power, authority and influence to change the world. May we walk through life's journey with wisdom in knowing this truth, "It's all about You!" Amen.

SCRIPTURE FOR DEEPER INSIGHT

[1] Psalm 23:3
[2] Joshua 14:12
[3] Malachi 3:2-3

REFLECTIONS

In loneliness and difficult seasons, we are wise to lean into our Shepherd to walk us through the storms. How do we do this? Listed below are "Six-By's" to consider:

- By being constantly aware of His presence and assured of His love.
- By talking to Him from the depth of our being, sharing the pain, hurt, confusion, anxiety and weakness we are experiencing.
- By reading scripture to find words of encouragement, rescue, teachings, and guidance.
- By listening to and obeying His promptings in next steps forward, even when His ways do not align with our wishes or desires. It's okay to ask Him for confirmation of His direction. He is not a God of confusion and does not get mad when we ask Him to confirm or repeat His promptings or directions.
- By spending time with Christian friends who speak truth and wisdom into our situation.
- By believing, no matter what, God has our best interests at heart and teaches us through the journey.

Day Sixteen

GOD'S SEA OF LOVE

"Above all, love each other deeply." 1 Peter 4:8

Before his seventeenth birthday, he invited me to dinner for a private conversation. He was peaceful and did not hesitate to share with me because of my love for God. I had been his spiritual mentor for years, leading him to Christ, attending his baptism, and often praying over him. We were close. When he gathered the courage, he told me, "I am gay." I quickly searched my heart. This lifestyle had been a conundrum for years, as it went against what I was taught to believe, yet those teachings seemed contrary to God's greatest commandment, which is to "love God and love others."[1]

He asked if I was angry. "I love you. I have watched you grow for many years and I am not surprised by your news." I took a breath and continued, "I know how people would tell me to respond, but I need to take this to the Lord and see how He would have me respond." This young man's answer, "I would not expect anything differently."

The next morning, I asked, "Lord, how do I respond? How do You feel? I have vocalized in the past, love the sinner, hate the sin. But that now feels judgmental and cold. I know the politics and religion around this issue. But Lord, I want to give him Your answer that comes from being in relationship with You. I do not want to give the opinion of others or answers that come through religious teaching."

As I stood in the presence of God, I sensed His Spirit come over me. It was as though God lifted me and placed me in the depths of the ocean. All around was His love. It enveloped me, held me close, kept me secure, as if placed in a womb. The height and depth were overwhelming, and I didn't want to be removed from His secure hold.

I heard His gentle voice answer, "Tell him My love for him is greater than he will ever know. I love him yesterday, today and tomorrow. Tell him to memorize Psalm 139 so he is assured of My love. Others will revolt against him, even those who proclaim to be my followers will tell him I am angry, he is not worthy of My love, and he is an abomination. When others rise and say these things, he needs to be grounded in My truth. I am always at work in his life, even when you can't see or understand. I have a purpose and plan. Your role as a believer is to love and pray for him; to continue to point him to Me; to share with him My words and goodness. Share My love with him and allow Me to complete the work."

Immediately, my viewpoint was secure. God is love. He is able to draw every person to Himself, in His way, in His timing. Our role is to love. Unconditionally. To pray for those who do not know God, to point them to His love, and to speak the truth as God directs. Our role is never to condemn, judge, or ridicule. There's enough of that without Christians falling into the same mindset and trap! God's love draws the broken and the lost. His love is enough. The same love God has for this young man, He has for me. He has for you. His love is unfathomable, untouchable, unshakable, unimaginable.[3] It is life-changing, transforming, pure and deep.

PRAYER

Father,

Help me love deeply, to show unconditional love to my spouse, children, parents, siblings, co-workers, and friends. When the spirit of religion rises in me, may I see it immediately and humble myself. May I not judge or ridicule others who live alternative life styles, but may I be an example of your love and grace. May I remember we live from the inside out, so the outward appearance is not reality. Let me be a walking example of your love, acceptance, forgiveness and grace. Amen.

SCRIPTURE FOR DEEPER INSIGHT

[1] Luke 12:30-31
[2] Ephesians 3:18

REFLECTIONS

Have you experienced God's love in a life-changing way? If not, ask God to give you a sense of His love and presence.

If you find you have bias against any people group or lifestyle, or if you judge people based on their outward appearance, confess these things to God and ask Him to give you His heart of love for all people.

THE BACKSIDE OF A BEAST

*"For I know that what has happened will turn
out for my deliverance."* Philippians 1:19

Our pastor called it a pilgrimage to Israel, walking the steps of Jesus and seeing the landscape where He preached and performed miracles. Every stop along the way was emotionally charged as we read the lessons and parables Jesus taught in each place. We dined by the Sea of Galilee, dipped our toes in the Jordan River, and relaxed on the Mount of Olives. We touched the Western Wall in Jerusalem's Old City and prayed in the Garden of Gethsemane. We walked the path to Golgotha, and we celebrated our rich heritage of being grafted into the family of Christ.[1]

The pilgrimage was a gift in every way. Because I worked at the church and was responsible for coordinating the travel plans, my expenses were covered. The timing of the trip was also a gift. My marriage was in collapse and my emotions were unraveling. The Holy Land beckoned, "Come," and my broken heart longed for the comfort of being in the land of miracles.

As I boarded the plane to Israel, I was keenly aware of the heavy burden I carried. Had it been weighable, it would have tipped the scales and been thrown from the plane. But the weight of emotional baggage can be camouflaged with a smile, and I was determined to hide my pain for the duration of the trip.

Fortunately, my camouflage worked, and my pain went unnoticed. That is, until a few days into the trip when our tour bus stopped at a shop in the Judea Desert. Happy to have a break from the rugged backroads of Israel, I stepped off the bus to look at the countryside. This was when my friend approached with an offer, "I just paid for you to ride a camel." I responded, "I don't want to ride a camel." "Well, I paid three dollars and they won't give me my money back." *Sigh.*

As I approached the platform to board the mammal, a young man held out his hand to offer assistance. He looked into my eyes and said, "Riding the camel will help your broken heart." My eyes welled with tears. How did this stranger see my inner pain? My emotional camouflage must have rubbed off. I carefully mounted the humpy bumpy backside of the camel and quickly learned he was right. The bouncy ride brought giggles and delight as I waved to onlookers, "hootie-hooing" around the parking lot, sitting atop mammal-the-camel. I have since learned, in the prophetic, a camel symbolizes God's provision. On a hot day in the desert, God gave me encouragement for the days ahead by putting me on the backside of a beast. He reminded me the pain within was not invisible to Him, and He assured me He would restore my joy.

Don't miss the hidden sermon. God cares for you. He places people in your path to give a word of encouragement or a helping hand. He orchestrates your life events to bring good from the bad. He provides for you in ways you may not see until you have hindsight vision. Every step of life, His outreached hand beckons, "Come." Will you take His hand and allow Him to delight you with His provision of love, understanding, and guidance?

PRAYER

Father,

Thank You. Whether in poverty or wealth, You provide for all my needs.[2] You sit with me in the depths when I grieve. You climb with me to the heights in my seasons of abundance. You provide for my physical needs, You restore my emotional wellness, You wrap me in spiritual blessings, and You invite me into Your heart through worship. You are my "enough," Lord. Amen.

SCRIPTURE FOR DEEPER INSIGHT

[1] Romans 11:17, John 15:5
[2] Proverbs 30:8-9

REFLECTIONS

When has God met you at a low point and shown you His love and provision?

Have you shared stories of God's faithfulness with others? Why or why not?

When you are in need, accept offers of help and provision from family and friends, understanding God often uses others to meet the needs of His children.

Day Eighteen

TOUCHING JESUS

"Then He touched me and raised me to my feet." Daniel 8:18

There she stood, alone on a cobblestone walkway in Bethlehem, waiting for the group so we could return to Jerusalem. As I approached, I saw her eyes filled with tears. She was ill and afraid she would have to return home and miss out on the remainder of the pilgrimage. She asked, "Can you please pray for God to heal me?" Why did she ask me? Probably because I was the first person she saw in her distress. I don't know. I never asked.

Nevertheless, here I was, standing face to face with her in the city where Jesus was born. I was insecure and broken, carrying my own heartbreak and praying for my own miracle. I was no stranger to fear and desperation. The look in her eyes mirrored my own, as I wrapped her in my arms, placed my lips next to her ear, and whispered a prayer for healing. The prayer was for both of us.

As I prayed, I heard the others approaching. They passed and noisily boarded the bus, calling out it was time to leave. But this prayer could not be hurried nor interrupted. Something was happening. I could sense the stirring of the Spirit and didn't want to release her until God prompted me the work was complete. I didn't voice any of this to my friend. Healing is God's work. He invited me to participate by holding and praying for her, but whatever was going on inside her body was all Him.

The next morning, I saw her in the restaurant. She reported, "God performed a miracle. As soon as we got back to the hotel, the pain was gone. I had a good night's sleep, I called my doctor and he advised me to stay." Another miracle performed in Bethlehem, the town of David.[1] Her miracle was given immediately; my miracle would be a work in progress.

LESSONS OF A DRAGONFLY | 69

After we returned home, she asked if I would pray over her daughter who was having difficulty conceiving a child. Miracles belong to the Lord. In scripture, Jesus asked the question, "Did I not tell you that if you believed, you would see the glory of God?"[2] I believe. As I prayed over her daughter, the Lord showed me she would give birth to twins. Ten months later, I greeted her newborn children.

During that season, my Bethlehem friend continued to send people for prayer and God allowed me to be part of many miracles. I didn't perform the miracles; my role was to pray as the Holy Spirit directed.[3]

The lesson impressed on my heart is for everyone to hear. Pray without fear, pray without worrying about the results, pray with faith that Man's impossibility is God's reality![4] He is our miracle God. When He touches us, things happen. Sometimes miracles are immediate; other times, they are a work in progress. Don't be afraid to ask someone to pray for your healing. And don't be afraid to pray for the healing of others. If you believe, you will see the glory of God.

PRAYER

Lord,

You are our Healer, our Great Physician. Touch us and make us whole. Jesus, in Your name, we rebuke infection, disease, and sickness and command it to leave. We speak health and strength into our body, lungs, bloodstream, and immune system. We speak healing into all organs, tissue, and bones in Jesus' name, and command them to return to normal functioning. We rebuke all pain and discomfort and command it to go. Father, we thank You for completely healing us. We believe. Help our unbelief. Amen.

SCRIPTURE FOR DEEPER INSIGHT

[1] Luke 2:4-7
[2] John 11:40
[3] Romans 8:26-27
[4] Mark 10:27

REFLECTIONS

Have you felt the touch of Jesus in your life? Perhaps through His Spirit or the touch or words of someone? Journal about this, expressing thanks to God. If not, write a prayer asking God to meet you in this way.

Have you experienced fear when asked to pray for another? How does this story encourage you to step out in faith and pray with boldness?

Day Nineteen

SURRENDER

*"Create in me a clean heart, O God, and renew
a right spirit within me."* Psalm 51:10

It was the last night of our pilgrimage in Israel, and I did not look forward to the trip home. Many decisions impacting our family for all eternity awaited. It was clear the way forward involved change and broken dreams. I dreaded the flight home knowing my ten-day absence had given my husband time to formulate his thoughts about our future. By his words and actions, he had forewarned me our marriage was over.

Unable to sleep, I made my way to the balcony overlooking the beautiful city of Jerusalem. I wondered how many people came to the Holy Land and unloaded their emotional baggage. I was reminded how, in this region, Jesus gave His life so I could live in freedom. I envisioned Jesus with me on the balcony, assuring me the road ahead would be a struggle, but I would not walk it alone.

As I sat in His presence, I prayed,

> "Lord, You brought me to Your beautiful land of Israel, to Jerusalem, Your city on a hill.[1] Thank You for the invitation and the provision to come. Lord, at this altar, I leave my broken heart, broken by me, broken by others. Healed only by You. I no longer desire to carry this brokenness, this burden, this sadness, this bent toward allowing others to define me. Show me who You have created me to be and return me to my destiny. Burn away negative strongholds blocking my way forward. Burn away any idol so You are my only God. May I know and stand strong in You. May my life be a sweet incense, as You burn away the unlovely,

the unholy, the broken. Lord, move me to a higher plane with You and allow me to see life through Your eyes and glorify You only. Amen."

Surrender is not easy. It requires humility and releasing the attitude of "I can do it myself." It beckons us to trust God with our life, our circumstances, and our relationships.[2] Often, we must come to our wits' end before surrender comes. Even then, surrender is like an onion with many layers, the first being the hardest to remove.

Once I surrendered my burden to Christ, I left the outer layer in Jerusalem. At the time, it was the only one I could see. Since then, I have dropped peelings all over the world. With every message I've delivered, another layer has been revealed and surrendered to God. Some layers are harder to release as they provide security and a covering, and shedding them feels too risky.

Often, in my mind, I am back on the balcony in Jerusalem, talking with Jesus, working through another area of surrender. That's what the journey of life is about. Walking with God. Working through issues one by one. Surrendering our will, our hurts, our desires so He can take away the not-so-good and give us His best. It's a great exchange.

PRAYER

Father,

May I continue this journey of prayer, seeking You daily, inviting You into my thoughts, my behaviors, attitudes, and motives. May I continually submit to You and be quick to confess my weaknesses, inviting You to teach me the better way and give me strength. May my tongue be used to praise You rather than curse others. May I be quick to love and forgive. Help me see life from Your perspective rather than my often limited and selfish view. Amen.

SCRIPTURE FOR DEEPER INSIGHT

[1] Matthew 5:14
[2] Romans 12:1-2
[3] Galatians 2:20

REFLECTIONS

Surrender. The act is a step of spiritual growth.[3] What do you hold tightly? Will you allow God to reveal it, so you can begin peeling back layers, releasing them, and becoming the person God destined you to be? It's a question worth considering.

What does the word, "surrender" stir within you? Fear and weakness? Strength and courage? What makes you feel this way?

Journal a prayer, asking God to help you understand how to surrender your will to His.

Day Twenty

PRAYING IT FORWARD

"We walk by faith, not by sight." 2 Corinthians 5:7

Life was messier with each passing day. I wanted to escape and be free from the voices telling me, "You're not enough." My marriage was in collapse, and I couldn't stop the pain from the unwanted breakup. To further complicate matters, I was scheduled as keynote speaker for a weekend conference, and cancellation was out of the question. I set about the task of preparing the message, but words of living water were far from my parched soul. I prayed, "Lord, I am void. I have nothing to give, no message to deliver." Yet, I had His peace.

At the conference, the first speaker shared her testimony, and closed with a question. "What in your life has left you breathless? Storms rip us apart. But remember, God puts the super in our natural; He puts the extra in our ordinary." I listened intently, feeling vulnerable and inadequate. I had been ripped apart and needed the super and the extra. I was a total mess, breathless and undone, when I was invited to the podium to deliver the message everyone, including myself, waited to hear. As I stood before the audience, my mind was blank. After several awkward seconds, words came, so I spoke as they were given. I shared the story of how Caleb said to Joshua, "Give me my mountain."[1] I continued, "After I prayed that same prayer, the enemy attacked with weapons of mass destruction to take possession of my God-given promise. I was defeated, standing as a victim at the bottom of a pit, looking up at the enemy, ready to surrender."

The words continued, "Rather than looking at life circumstances from a position of defeat, we are called out of the pit." I jumped onto the fireplace hearth, about two feet above the floor, and took the stance of a warrior. The Holy Spirit had hold as the words continued. "In every battle, we are victorious in Christ[2]. We stand with Him, looking down on our enemies. When we cannot see God's work in the natural realm, we are assured He is working in the spiritual realm. We take our eyes off sight and we put them in faith, praying the promises of God forward. Not from a place of victim, but from a place of victor, with faith and thanksgiving for what God is doing."

In praying God's promise forward, we stay a step ahead of our circumstances, seeing through God's perspective rather than in the natural realm. We advance as our prayers advance. We continually pray our situation forward into God's Will and promise. We don't pray the problem; we pray the promise. For example, use God's promise, "I work all things together for good."[3] We are assured no matter what comes against us, God will use it for our good and His glory, if we walk in His ways. When tragedy strikes, we pray, "God, teach me through this and use this for Your glory." With every weapon set against us, we counter it with faith that God is at work and the battle is victorious. We battle with prayer, from a place of victory, never a place of defeat, never from the stance of "woe is me."

PRAYER

Lord,

Thank you for leading me through this battle. Often, I feel defeated, disappointed, and ready to surrender. Give me strength and faith to stand in a position of victory. May faith be bigger than my eyesight. May I see life from your perspective, which sees all time, all history, all situations, and circumstances. Open my eyes to the spiritual workings taking place within my situation. Let me see how you are battling on my behalf, teach me to pray your promises forward in life's circumstances. Lord, give me understanding of this spiritual truth. It is difficult to comprehend, yet, I know you go ahead of us to prepare the way, and you call us to go ahead of life's circumstances to prepare the way in prayer. Amen.

SCRIPTURE FOR DEEPER INSIGHT

[1] Joshua 14:10-12
[2] 1 Corinthians 15:57
[3] Romans 8:28
[4] Cowman, Mrs. Charles E. *Streams in the Desert*. Grand Rapids: Zondervan, 1997

REFLECTIONS

> *"Only say you have what God says you have, and He will make good to you all you believe. Only it must be real faith, all there is in you must go over in that act of faith to God."* [4]

Have you experienced the Holy Spirit giving you words to speak or pray? Explain. If not, remember, God gives words and wisdom when you ask.

Is there a situation in life where you feel defeated? Ask God to give you a promise from His Word to apply to your situation. Begin praying through your situation, applying this promise from God. Ask Him to show you His perspective and teach you to pray His promise forward. Invite Him, "Lord, teach me to pray."

Day Twenty-One

THE GIFT

"Whatever you did for one of the least of these,
you did for me." Matthew 25:40-45

Two months before his high school graduation, Patrick asked to borrow the car. His best friend was suffering from depression and threatening to take his life. Rather than giving Patrick the car keys, his father and I drove him around the area, looking for his friend. After hours of unsuccessful searching, we returned home. The next morning, we received the dreaded phone call. The pain of sharing the news with our son sent us to our knees, pleading with God to be his lifeline.

Patrick went into deep depression and there was nothing we could do to ease his pain. So, we did what we knew. We invited his friends over. We encouraged him to eat. We prayed. We cried. We sat in devastation with him. We knew it was on him to find the emotional and spiritual tools to handle the acceptance and healing. We could introduce him to the tools; but he had to grab and use them.

After Patrick's high school graduation, my husband and I separated. Further devastation piled into Patrick's already broken heart. A month later, we dropped him off at his college dorm. Though distanced by a three-hour drive, Patrick and I were closely connected, and I could feel his pain melding with mine. He was raw from news of death and divorce. Now he was off to college to make a new life for himself. Who does that to a kid? He was not ready for this added stress. Shortly into his college experience, I received a call. "Mom, I have a fever, my skin is yellow, and I have a sore throat. Will you come get me?" Patrick was admitted to the hospital with mononucleosis and burst tonsils. This should have been a wake-up call. After his hospital release, he returned to school. When he came home for Christmas break, Patrick was thirty pounds lighter, and looked like a skeleton tightly wrapped in skin. He had an eating disorder and entered a behavioral health hospital for several weeks.

After release, he stayed home to heal, physically, emotionally, mentally and spiritually. I was relieved to have him home, as we both needed deep healing, and working through the process together was the next step forward. There was only one problem. Because I worked full-time, Patrick was alone during the day. He needed the distraction of friends or a job, but I didn't have the financial means to buy him a car. Winter depression hovered, and I worried for his life. God sent a close friend to do a wellness check. Before leaving, she handed me an envelope and said, "Patrick needs to get out of the house and be with people, or you will lose him. Use this money to buy him a vehicle." Who, other than family, does that for a kid? She heard from God and obeyed His promptings. I have no doubt her gift saved his life and helped him on his road to recovery. Seven years later, Patrick sent me this message, "Today is the anniversary of the dark times. I am better than I have ever been, and life is a blessing again. Thank you for being there for me when life was rough." God says, "Behold I make all things new."[1] He did, and He does.

PRAYER

Father,

Thank You for Your abiding presence. You watch over us throughout our lives. You provide emotional, spiritual, and mental tools to help us walk through the dark days, and to share with others as they walk through dark days. Lord, be our guide. Be our stronghold. Be our life support. May we call on You in our days of despair and devastation. May we be willing to sit with others in their silent place of despair. Teach us, Lord, to be a comfort. Compel us to help others in Your way, even when it means giving from our lack instead of from our plenty. All we have is Yours, Lord. Help us share our blessings with those in need. Who knows when our gift, given out of obedience to You, will save a life! Amen.

SCRIPTURE FOR DEEPER INSIGHT

[1] Revelation 21:5
Matthew 25:40-45
Matthew 5:3
Luke 6:38

REFLECTIONS

Life is fragile. Hold those who are heartbroken and don't be too quick to move them into activities before they have an opportunity to catch their breath and grieve their pain. Be sensitive to the Holy Spirit's leading.

Listed below are tools you can use to minister to those who are heartbroken and devastated. Read the verses associated with each one. Add more tools as the Holy Spirit brings them to mind.

> The ministry of presence. This is the ability to sit quietly with someone, grieving with them without using words, giving advice, or trying to cheer them with empty stories. (Job 2:13)

> The ministry of prayer. If they ask, pray for and with them in the moment. Don't delay or say, "I'm praying for you." If sitting in silence, pray over them, quietly, lifting them to God, inviting His presence to hover and comfort. (Ephesians 6:18)

Day Twenty-Two

NO STRINGS ATTACHED

"Give, and it will be given to you." Luke 6:38

The woman needed a bedroom suite, and I had one to give. The Red Cross needed blood for hurricane victims, so I offered a vein. A friend needed a kidney, so I donated one. The little boy was blind in one eye, so I lifted a prayer. The teenage girl needed a place to heal, so I provided a bed, meals, a listening ear and open arms. No strings attached. Love led the way. You get the gist. We each have stories of how gifts and donations have changed our life and the lives of those we love. Yet, giving doesn't always come naturally. For some, the idea of sharing is a foreign concept; for others, it's a genuine overflow of the heart. But once tried, scripture is proven true, "It is more blessed to give than to receive."[1]

When I was a girl, my parents opened our home for my aunt and cousins to stay for a season. I learned about the gift of hospitality and sharing what one has, even when it's not much. There w ere n o s trings attached. Love led the way. Years later, my sister opened her home to a two-year old boy. At first, he was a playmate for her son. The two boys became best friends and were inseparable. As the boys grew, they became more like brothers, attending church and youth events together. The "brothers" were baptized on the same day, which was the beginning of the young boy's family returning to church. My sister became his "other mother," his "home away from home." Her heart and home were opened to embrace a young boy who needed the security of a brother and the stability of a second family. Her unconditional love for him was a natural overflow of the heart, no strings attached.

During my days of brokenness, I could not discern the way forward. Was I to stay in Illinois or move home to Texas? In the fog of confusion, I gave up the lease on my rental property and needed short-term housing.

A couple from church invited me to move into their home while I determined my next steps. No strings attached. Love led the way. They hosted me for several months which provided the opportunity to steady my emotions before making decisions.

Our words and actions are pushed into the world in seed form, planted in a field of fertile soil.[2] Will your field produce a harvest of beauty or yield a crop of thorns? We plant good seeds in a field of unconditional love, nourish with thanksgiving, water with God's grace, all of which produce seed bearing fruit.[3] No strings attached. Isn't that better than looking back at life and seeing a field of thorns and thistles, planted in the soil of greed, fertilized with unforgiveness and bitterness, watered by indifference, yielding a harvest of emptiness?

Let us be known as those who sow generosity instead of greed; kindness instead of hostility; contentment instead of dissatisfaction. Rather than measuring our generosity with a spoon, let us give "A good measure, pressed down, shaken together and running over."[4] No strings attached.

PRAYER

Father,

May I honor You with the same generosity You show me by giving to those in need. Whether it be a gift of finances, a kind word or worn coat, grocery money, or honor and respect. May I give generously to Your Kingdom without worry that what remains will not stretch far enough. May I never look to Man to fill the needs that only You can meet, and may I use the resources You so freely give in the way that honors You and increases Your Kingdom. Lord, may I be generous rather than greedy. May I share rather than hoard. May I represent You in all areas of my life, whether I have much or little. Amen.

SCRIPTURE FOR DEEPER INSIGHT

[1] Acts 20:35
[2] Galatians 6:7-8

[3] John 15:16
[4] Luke 6:38

REFLECTIONS

It is good to do a heart-check annually. Is there anything you consider more valuable than the things of God? Open your hand and release what you hold tightly, whether it is finances, your time or possessions. Ask God to use that "one thing" to bring joy to another.

Examine your life to determine if you are currently reaping what you may have sown in years past. Take a fresh look at your spiritual farmland and seed packets. Do you need to exchange hostility for kindness? Anger for gentleness? Greed for generosity? Gossip for prayerfulness? Begin now planting seeds for your future harvest.

Day Twenty-Three

UPSIDE DOWN

"I want Your will to be done, not mine." Luke 22:42

When my husband and I separated, my heart broke; when he filed for divorce, it died. Every decision he made carried him further from our family, yet there was nothing I could do to change the situation. I desperately wanted someone to pray him home, so I met with a pastor. After I explained the situation, the pastor prayed, "Father, thank You for Mary's husband. I pray blessings over his decisions, that they will positively impact his life. I pray blessings over his faith, that he will come to know You in a real and intimate way. May his eyes focus on You, as you lead him through his journey. Bless his career, his finances, his faith, and his children. Keep him safe, protected, and let him know he is loved by You. Amen."

To say the least, I was surprised. The pastor did not pray as expected, nor did he pray the man home. Could it be, he was entrusting the decisions and direction of my husband's life into the hands of God? Perhaps I needed to do the same; pray a blessing over him and release him. In hindsight, I realize my motive was to find someone to manipulate God into answering my prayer in my way. What was my way? For God to awaken his senses and put him back with the family. I was operating out of fear, of course. The marriage was my identity, and without it, I was lost.

Again, hindsight shows God's wisdom. Because my identity was lost in a co-dependent marriage, sense of Self vanished. The break in the marriage put me on a journey to reclaim the person God created me to become. It was not an easy journey, yet it was rewarding. Learning to engage in present life, leaving the past behind, was a great challenge. Being reminded of who I am apart from other people and relationships has been an ongoing gift, though lonely at times. Intentionally deciding to live as a single adult was key in understanding who I am apart from anyone else. Part of the journey to wholeness is learning to develop community without the help of children or a spouse. I have learned I am complete, even without a mate. What a miracle.

I appreciate the pastor's prayer more today than ever. His example stays with me. Often people ask for prayer and tell me specifically how to pray. I recognize prayer attempts to manipulate God, since I had the same thoughts at one time. Yet I follow the example of my pastor-friend and pray a blessing over the situation, trusting God has everything under control.

When our lives are turned upside down and we have nowhere to go, no control over the situation, no way to turn back the clock, God puts us on a new path and shows us abundant living we would not have known without the desperate sense of brokenness. He loves us and works beauty from our ashes of despair.

PRAYER

Father,

Increase my trust in You. Reveal the wrong motives desiring to manipulate and control others, including You. Teach me the upside-down ways of Your teaching to "Love my enemies, do good to those who hate me, bless those who curse me, and pray for those who mistreat me." Help me repay evil with kindness and not take revenge in my own hands. Mature me in Your ways and help me see hardship and brokenness as an opportunity to become stronger in my walk with You. May my prayers be filled with grace and forgiveness. You have called me higher in thoughts, actions and responses. Keep me in alignment with You. May I have wisdom and strength to bless those who come against me. May my life reflect my love and devotion to Christ. Amen.

SCRIPTURE FOR DEEPER INSIGHT

1 Corinthians 13:8
Romans 8:28
Luke 6:27-31

REFLECTIONS

In your season of brokenness, how has God shown Himself faithful? How have you changed because of heartbreak? If you are currently in a season of brokenness, remember, God sees you, knows you, and goes ahead of you, preparing your steps for joy to return.

Read Luke 6:27-31. How does God's upside-down way of living challenge you? (Bless those who curse you, turn the other cheek.)

Day Twenty-Four

QUESTIONS AND ANSWERS

"Is anything too hard for the Lord?" Genesis 18:14

Often, we look at life's circumstances and doubt God's ability or willingness to bring about change. Other times, we don't want to do the work of changing Self, so we work to change or control others. We decide within our humanity that our prayers are futile, we don't want to waste God's time with our requests, or we fail to invite Him into the situation, thinking we can handle life apart from Him.

All God's promises will be fulfilled, in His way and His time. The problems and challenges come in our attitude because we do not believe. So, we question, "Did God really say?" "Does He really mean…?" We measure God's love, trustworthiness and faithfulness on human scales. We see the shortcomings, failures, and flaws of mortal companions and relate those to God. Then we decide the only one we can count on is Self, so we discount God's power and plan. Not only do we ask the questions, we assume we know the answers, and life continues along the road called Faithless and Disbelief. It would behoove us to lean into the Lord to glean knowledge and understanding of life's predicaments and plights.

In scripture, God uses questions to teach deep truths we might otherwise miss. He also provides the answers. He asks, "Is anything too hard for the Lord?"[1] He answers, "Nothing is impossible with God."[2] He asks, "Is the Lord's arm too short?"[3] He answers, "I will give you the treasures of darkness, riches stored in secret places."[4]

Is God able and willing to change our circumstances? Does He hear our requests? Are we wasting His time praying about our needs?

The answers are found in scripture. "The prayer of a righteous man is powerful and effective."[5] "Call to me and I will answer and tell you great and unsearchable things."[6] Our prayers have power to bring about change.

It is His plan that we invite Him into life's mysteries and messes. Don't believe it? Ask Him for guidance, then devote time to sit, fellowship, and listen to Him. You will be amazed.

God created us to be in relationship with Him and He desires our companionship. Asking questions and waiting for answers is one element of growing in our faith and enriching our understanding of Him. May we settle our minds on these truths and open our heart to pray for those seemingly impossible things. May we continually bring Him the cares and stresses of life, trusting Him to give insight and wisdom in moving forward. Let us keep our focus on what God is doing in response to our prayers. Remember, our impossibility is God's reality!

PRAYER

Father,

Give me clarity of thought, bathed in Your truth that shines the light in the darkness of my mind where the lies of Satan hide. Lies telling me You are too busy to care about the details of my life; lies hindering me from bringing requests to You. Your truth says You care about every detail of my life, whether great or small, and You have all the time in the world to listen and talk. I desire intimacy with You, Lord. Teach me to draw near, to trust, and to abide in You. Amen.

SCRIPTURE FOR DEEPER INSIGHT

[1] Genesis 18:14
[2] Luke 1:37
[3] Numbers 11:23
[4] Isaiah 45:3
[5] James 5:16
[6] Jeremiah 33:3

REFLECTIONS

Do you doubt God's ability or desire to meet your needs? Why or why not?

List your greatest worries or concerns. Pray, "Lord, I lay these things at your feet, trusting you to work them out. Help me listen to you, obey your promptings, and stay out of Your way unless You ask for my help. Amen." Repeat this prayer as often as necessary to release these to God.

Day Twenty-Five

CAPTIVATED BY JESUS

"She fell at his feet." John 11:32

When we first meet Mary of Bethany, she is a student, sitting at the feet of Jesus, taking in every word.[1] Later, we find Mary at His feet, crying inconsolably.[2] Days earlier, she sent word for Jesus to come because her brother, Lazarus, was sick. Yet He waited. In the wait, Lazarus died and was laid to rest. In the wait, Mary's heart and mind were burdened with processing and reasoning through the what, why, and how of the death of Lazarus and the delay of Jesus. In these days of waiting, she was a prime target for Satan to taunt with lies of betrayal. These were long days to sit in the pain of her raw, confused and crushed heart. Why did the One who could bring healing delay appearing? Her life was surrendered to Him, yet, He was nowhere to be found. She was overtaken by grief and vanishing hope. She didn't know how to stop the pain and there was nowhere to lay her burden.

Then she saw Jesus. Her Burden-Bearer. The One who gives love, security and comfort. She was filled with hope as she crumbled at His feet, worshipping the only One who could make sense of her brother's death. She emptied herself of every raw emotion, crying, "Lord, if you had been here, my brother would not have died."

Her tears and grief stirred the heart of Jesus, causing Him to weep with her. Then, He lifted her to her feet and asked, "Did I not tell you that if you believed, you would see the glory of God?" He understood Mary's grief. He sensed her desperate hope. He also knew her heart of worship and love for Him. And He knew His Heavenly Father was going to bring restoration through a miracle.

In your mind's eye, can you see the love in His eyes as He walked toward the tomb and asked for the stone to be rolled away? Imagine the authority in His voice as He trampled death and called, "Lazarus, come out!" Hear the gasps, delight, squeals, laughter, and amazement of the people, including Mary and her sister, Martha, as the dead man rose to his feet and walked out of the tomb.

And just like that, Mary's raw heart was healed. Instantaneously. With one command from Jesus, her joy was restored, her faith made whole. What was her response to Jesus? The next time she is mentioned in scripture, she is expressing her worship and devotion by anointing His feet with perfume.[4]

Where do we go for comfort? We follow the example of Mary and we crumble at the feet of Jesus. Through the power of laying all things at His feet-grief, worries, and fears-we hear His voice speaking into our heart, "Did I not tell you that if you believed, you would see the glory of God?" His resurrection power restores a hemorrhaging heart to health and delights us in the promise He works all things to our greatest benefit.[5]

PRAYER

Father,

Increase my faith. Give me the desire to sit at Your feet, to be a student, a worshiper, a believer of Your miracles. When life is difficult, may I bring my grief and pain to You, entrusting my heart and emotions to You for comfort and peace. May I never place judgment or blame on You for the hardships. May I always look to You, trusting You to work all things to my greatest benefit. Lord, may I decrease in self-will, so my life will fully reflect You. Amen.

SCRIPTURE FOR DEEPER INSIGHT

[1] Luke 10:38-42
[2] John 11:1-44
[3] John 12:3
[4] Romans 8:28

REFLECTIONS

Can you relate to Mary of Bethany, crumbling at the feet of Jesus in grief and brokenness? Explain.

What are the things you turn to when you need comfort?

How has Jesus been your comfort when you have experienced a raw or broken heart?

Day Twenty-Six

·+·◆◆◆·+·

THE RAW HEART

*"He set my feet upon a rock and gave me
a firm place to stand."* Psalm 40:2

What is a raw heart? It is a heart beaten, vulnerable, exposed and torn to shreds, homesick for something that was, yet will never be again. Loss and devastation hit the heart like a mallet, pounding emotions to shreds, tearing away the protective covering of security, family, significance, identity, future and hope.

What remains? A heart, unprotected and afraid, linked to the past with no desire to face the future, sustained only by the breath of God. It seeks relief from pain that cannot be escaped. It plunges to the depth of the soul, saturating in nothingness, not caring to climb out. It calls to God from the depth, seeking assurance of His unconditional love, and desires only to marinate in His presence, knowing He alone holds comfort. The Holy Spirit comes and sits with the one in pain, holding them, whispering, "Everything is going to be okay. Rest, child. Grieve, child. Release your pain to Me. We will walk through this together, and when the pain is too great, I will carry you."

The pain inflicted on the raw heart demands answers. What did I miss? Did I do enough? What could I have done to prevent this? Gently and slowly, God provides understanding. Though He does not always provide the answers requested, He gives what is needed to bring healing to the raw heart, and He opens the way forward. It is in the raw heart God does His greatest work. Why? Because the raw heart desperately seeks understanding of things not of this world. Answers only God can provide. In the depth of the soul, God works miracles.[1] Though broken, the heart is humble, teachable and searchable. Slowly the mind is opened to a new truth. Life is different now, and a new way needs to be forged. This understanding ushers in change.

Before the new life can be accepted, the old life must be peeled away, resolved, and healed. In solitude, courage is found to explore the raw heart. Though it fears what is shown, it moves into the depth, desperately searching for a way forward, to bring purpose to the loss, to gain a treasure from the pain. What is seen is alarming yet comforting. An ungodly character trait, wounds, hidden motives, or pain from the past is uncovered. Alas, something to surrender to God for refining, something to bring beauty from the loss. Something one can do to bring about purpose.

Eventually, the raw heart realizes God directs the path to a place of healing. He holds the raw heart in His hand, protecting it from further damage and breaking. His desire is to restore the heart to its original design, not encased in a hardened protective covering, but rather, guarded in the greatest covering of all – His love. God is close to the brokenhearted, He saves those who are crushed in spirit,[2] and He makes beauty from ashes.[3] He is a safe place; entrust your heart to Him and follow Him along the pathway of healing.

PRAYER

Father,

My heart is raw, torn to shreds by loss and devastation. Be my breath, my lifeline. Hold me in the grip of Your love and grace. Help me make sense of life, events, and things I cannot control nor reverse. Bring healing to my innermost parts. Restore my heart. As I sit in solitude with You, comfort me with Your presence, hold me with Your love. Help me grieve the loss, the sadness, the hopelessness. Show me how to walk forward when all I want to do is go into the past where life was familiar. Help me forgive myself for anything I may have missed along the way pointing me to this tragedy, help me process through this sadness, and hold my faith steady in You. I ask, Lord, hold me in this place of quiet and rest with You until I can face the world. Let me focus on caring for Self and others who are directly impacted by this loss, Lord. Help me understand it is okay to rein in my life for a season of grief and healing. There is no guilt in protecting

Self from further hurt or damage. Help me remember, Lord, healing is a work done with You. Hold me steady. Amen.

SCRIPTURE FOR DEEPER INSIGHT

[1] Psalm 147:3
[2] Psalm 34:18
[3] Isaiah 61:3

REFLECTIONS

If you are experiencing a raw heart, keep clinging to the One who holds you. Don't hesitate to connect with Him spirit to Spirit. His love covers you like a warm blanket and restores your passion for life.

If you have experienced a raw heart, may the Lord bless you and bring you complete wholeness and restoration. Through the days of your life, may you continually see God's hand bringing beauty from ashes.

Read the referenced scriptures. Sit with the words, allowing them to soak into your heart. If you have not experienced a raw heart, pray for others who have.

Day Twenty-Seven

BURDEN-BEARER

*"Bear one another's burdens, and so fulfill
the law of Christ."* Galatians 6:2

To heal from brokenness takes time, patience, and intentional living. There is a need to remind Self to breathe. To eat. To exercise. To will oneself out of bed each morning. Sorrow cannot be bypassed nor surgically removed. The pain cuts into the heart, and healing is a process. When sorrow comes, one has the choice in how to react to the pain. Accept it and work through it, or bury it deep within, only to have it surface later.

In my season of sorrow, I leaned heavily into the Lord to be my Shepherd who gathered me in His arms and carried me close to His bosom.[1] Yet, my raw heart also needed a Burden-Bearer made of flesh and blood. The pain of the mornings and evenings was too great. I needed someone to listen to my heartbreak and carry my burden to the Lord. Someone who would not judge nor try to fix me. Someone who would listen and pray, often at the same time.

Scripture tells us we are to bear one another's burdens, which means He must also have someone to bear ours. For me, it was an out-of-state acquaintance who called to say, "I know we don't know each other very well, but I think God wants me to walk you through this season." I knew immediately she was a safe place, a God-send. She sat for hours and listened as I poured out my pain. I did not plan on unloading my burden. I had no intention of entrusting my broken heart into her care. Yet when I reached out, she silently prayed. Even when I was unaware, she prayed.

Allowing her into my burden taught me a lesson we all need to understand. God often meets our needs through Burden-Bearers. Those who listen and pray, as the Holy Spirit leads. Those who, supernaturally,

LESSONS OF A DRAGONFLY | 105

lift the weight of the burden from us and carry it to the foot of the cross, leaving it there.

My Burden-Bearer served me for a year. She checked in regularly. She listened. She often called to tell me how the Lord was leading her in prayer. There were days the burden was too great for me to handle. I didn't tell her. She just knew. And she spent those days on her knees before the Lord, asking Him to give me strength to keep going. Over time, I learned the importance of her role and shared more of my hurts, pains, thoughts, and fears. She took everything to the Lord. She was my lifeline to Jesus and prayed me through life's toughest storm. I am forever grateful.

When you are in brokenness, ask the Lord to send you a Burden-Bearer. Someone who will listen[2], pray, and carry your burden to the cross. Someone who will hold your secrets in confidence. If God calls you to be a Burden-Bearer[3], here are a few suggestions: Be a confidant. Be available but set boundaries so your time commitment is not abused. Pray as prompted. Share your prayers with the brokenhearted person so they can see how God is directing you to pray. Pray with and for the brokenhearted until God gives you release. Remember, it is not your job to fix. Don't give advice; don't ask detailed questions. Listen, pray, release.

PRAYER

Lord,

Thank You for the gift of prayer and for those who are called to bear the burdens of others. May I never take for granted the ones who pray for me, nor the promptings from You to pray for another. Bind the brokenhearted, Lord. Send comfort through words, songs, and the presence of Your followers. You are our Burden-Bearer, yet we know You also use others to be our lifeline to You when our hearts are too weak and raw to carry our own burden. Thank You for being all we need in life. Let us daily look to You to bring provision, healing, comfort, and burden-bearers to carry our heavy load when we cannot carry it on our own. Amen.

SCRIPTURE FOR DEEPER INSIGHT

[1] Isaiah 40:11
[2] Psalm 34:17
[3] Galatians 6:2

REFLECTIONS

Have you had someone pray for you in such a way you felt immediate comfort or sensed a lighter load? How did this grow your faith?

Has God called you to bear the burden of another? How did being a Burden-Bearer grow your faith?

Day Twenty-Eight

⋅⋅◆◆◆◆⋅⋅

INNER BEAUTY

"For we are God's workmanship." Ephesians 2:10

"She looks nice, but her clothes are from a thrift store, head to toe." I followed the gaze of my acquaintance. Indeed, the young woman in the thrift store clothes looked like a runway model, dressed to the nines, carrying herself in the same manner. I would never guess she wore secondhand clothes, yet knowing this gave me a sense of camaraderie with this woman I barely knew. Why?

Seventy-five percent of my attire was also secondhand, purchased at a local thrift store. Recently divorced and stretching finances had me cutting back in all areas. The stress of the marital situation caused me to drop two dress sizes, so adjustments had to be made for work attire. I kept quiet, not wanting to invite the same criticism into the gaping wound of being "not-enough." At this moment, I felt less than, insecure, a ragamuffin of sorts. Silence set in as I realized I did not meet the criteria and dressing nicely didn't matter if the clothes were used. A voice echoed from childhood, reminding me of truth, "It's the person that makes the clothes, not the clothes that make the person." The words were not enough to lift me above the judgment. Internally I cried out to God for His comfort, asking Him to remind me of my significance found in being His child. I had been through the emotional wringer in recent months and the sting of the criticizing words, though not directed at me, cut deep and hit an emotional nerve. In response to my prayer, God did two things.

First, He reminded me, "Man looks at the outward appearance, but I look at the heart."[1] Rather than crumble under the critical eye of Man, I was to clothe myself in the garments of Christ. "Clothe yourselves with compassion, kindness, humility, gentleness and patience. Forgive one another and put on love which binds them all together in perfect unity."[2]

These were firsthand clothes, designer-made, the finest the universe had to offer, and with a little time and practice, they would fit me to perfection and never wear out.

Second, He reminded me to consider the lilies.[3] "They do not labor or spin. Yet I tell you that not even Solomon in all his splendor was dressed like one of these." God desires for our character to be Christ-like. And He cares. He never wants His children to feel less-than, and often, He provides a blessing above anything we can imagine. His answer arrived a short time later. A friend invited me to her storefront to pick out several pieces of designer labels she no longer carried. God responded to my heart's cry in two ways – with tenderness and with treasure, ministering to both my inner and outer needs.

God cares about every detail of our lives and often lavishes us with gifts unimaginable and unexpected. If you find yourself in a place of need, tell Him, then watch and see how He responds.

PRAYER

Father,

On the days I feel less-than, not enough, and insecure, may my inner spirit pull You close. You are my "enough," my "security." I am Your design, created in Christ Jesus to walk with You. Help me see Self through Your eyes of love, purpose and uniqueness. Help me see others through Your eyes, remembering we all have days of insecurity, fear and feeling "less-than". May Your compassion flow through me for myself and for others, and may I not allow unmet expectations to be a blockage for Christ-like love to flow. Help me remember when I have a need, to call on You, knowing You will answer.[4] Amen.

SCRIPTURE FOR DEEPER INSIGHT

[1] I Samuel 16:7
[2] Colossians 3:12-14
[3] Matthew 6:28
[4] Jeremiah 33:3

REFLECTIONS

List any insecurities that limit your potential or make you feel "less-than."

How can you find significance through God in these areas? Consider scripture listed in this devotional as a first step in overcoming these negative thoughts.

Day Twenty-Nine

RISE AND GO

"Rise and go; your faith has made you well." John 17:19

Patty and her family live on a farm in upstate New York with a pond, a barn, a garden, and at last count, two dogs, a cat, and a pet pig. For several years, Patty hosted a one-day conference on the property. She transformed the barn into a meeting facility, she cut a labyrinth into the grass field atop a hill for quiet time reflection, and erected a cross in the middle. Patty recruited a team to assist with hospitality, decorations, and theatrical productions, and she invited me each year to be the event speaker. It was an anointed place and time.

One morning, as eighty women gathered for the first session, the worship leader approached. "I want you to pray for me after the conference. My children and I have food allergies, and I know we will be healed when you pray."

At the end of the conference, as darkness fell, women slowly made their exit. Privately, I hoped the worship leader would forget her plan as I was doubtful the Lord wanted to use me to pour out healing. (Oh ye, of little faith!)[1] She didn't forget. She found me, and escorted me to the front porch, out of sight of the others. We joined hands and prayed. After several minutes, she stood to her feet and said, "I have been healed. I need to go jump in the pond to seal the promise." I laughed. "You need to do what?"

The remaining women had gone into the house, so I joined the worship leader and walked to the pond. She walked to the edge of the dock and jumped in, feet first. She surfaced laughing hysterically. Something within was stirring, and she knew without hesitation her food allergies were gone from her and her children. A week later, she sent pictures of "the healed,"[2] enjoying a box of doughnuts. No more gluten intolerance.

I've questioned why she needed to "seal the promise." I believe it was

God's way of testing her faith – as He did when He sent the blind man to "wash in the Pool of Siloam."[3] As for me, it was not my faith that healed her. I simply obeyed the Lord and prayed the words He gave.[4] Through that experience, He reminded me of a valuable truth. It's not my job to "conjure" His presence or to work a miracle through my own power, though, a little faith on my part couldn't hurt.

What did I learn? No matter what we "feel," God can use us. We are to pray as He leads and leave the results to Him. In addition, it is not necessarily our role to second guess what He speaks to another faith-walking, Spirit-filled adult. Had I voiced my opinions, I would have warned the worship leader not to jump into the pond. It was dark, the water was cold, she couldn't see the surface and didn't know the depth. I kept silent and watched God use her faith to make her whole.[5] Jesus said, "If you believe, you will see the glory of the Lord."[6] Do you believe? Have you seen? Many times, the answer is at your disposal, waiting for the request to be made. Step out in faith. Ask and receive.

PRAYER

Father,

Thank You for the wisdom you speak into my spirit. Not only do You hear my words, You see my heart, know my anxious thoughts, and understand my weakness and struggles. Even when I don't have words to express my needs, You hear my cry. Even when I sit in Your presence in silence, releasing my troubles without words, You hear and give me peace. How can I express my gratitude? Even when I struggle, You continually pray for me to have strength, courage, freedom, healing, and victory! Be praised, Lord. Amen.

SCRIPTURE FOR DEEPER INSIGHT

[1] Matthew 6:30
[2] 1 Peter 2:24
[3] John 9:1-11
[4] Romans 8:34

[5] Luke 17:19
[6] John 11:40

REFLECTIONS

What step of faith have you taken to learn more of God's faithfulness?

Is there a fear holding you back from obedience to God's promptings? What is the remedy for this fear? Write a prayer, asking God for courage to overcome your fear.

Day Thirty

BE STILL AND KNOW

"If we ask according to His will, He hears it." 1 John 5:14

In scripture, we learn Jesus only spoke what God told Him to say,[1] and He only did what God told Him to do.[2] We have the same opportunity to speak and act as God leads. In prayer, the Holy Spirit leads us, so we ask in accordance with God's will, but we must be inclined to take the time, before prayer, to settle our spirit and listen. He gives words, pictures, or impressions of what to say. Sometimes He gives words that don't make sense to the one praying yet ministers to the one being prayed for. Praying in the way directed by the Holy Spirit guarantees answered prayer.[3] Below are two stories demonstrating promptings in prayer from the Holy Spirit.

One day, a friend called. Her young daughter was diagnosed with stage four cancer in the form of a tumor near her heart. She asked, "Can you and Martha come pray?" (Martha is my ministry partner.) On the way to visit our friend, I worried our prayers would not be enough. When we pulled into the driveway, fear urged me to cancel the plans and leave; love pushed me to the front door, and then into the home where the family waited.

As we gathered to pray, we closed our eyes, took a deep breath, and waited for the Holy Spirit to lead. Rather than giving words, the Holy Spirit showed me a slow-moving video.[4] I watched holy hands reach into the chest of this little girl, and gently massage her heart until the tumorous mass dissolved. Before I could question the vision, Martha prayed, "Lord Jesus, we ask for a miracle. Reach inside and touch this young girls' heart and dissolve the tumor." The Holy Spirit showed me His Will at the same time He gave Martha the words. With confidence we told the family, "God has granted a miracle that will be worked out through chemotherapy and radiation. Walk through the treatments without worry or fear. Your daughter is healed." (Yes, they received their miracle.)

One morning in a women's gathering, prayer was requested for the relationship between a mom and her teenage son. As I prayed, I caught the scent of apple cider. I surmised the smell was a prompting by the Holy Spirit and prayed, "Lord may the aroma of this family be like warm cider. May this boy be calmed when he is home, just as cider comforts us on a cold day."

After our prayer time, the mom pulled me aside and said, "Yesterday, I purchased a gallon of apple cider, thinking, 'My son loves warm cider. When he comes in from school, I'll make him a warm cup and we will start the afternoon off right.' However, when he arrived home, we settled into our routine and I never made the cider. This morning, we slept in, so no cider. When I left home, the thought crossed my mind to make the cider tonight." Her smile broadened, "I'll be sure to have that apple cider ready when he gets home." The mention of the comforting beverage in prayer confirmed to her God's work and watchfulness in the midst of their family storm.

Through a spiritual sense of smell, through visual imagery in our minds, through words given as we pray, the Holy Spirit teaches us how to intercede for others. Pay attention to the promptings. He never leads us astray.

PRAYER

Father,

Thank you for the way you love my family and the way you watch over my children. May I never hesitate to ask for prayer for healing, comfort, guidance, or even patience. Help me love my children with a heart like Yours. Help me raise them and correct their behavior in a way that prepares them to become young men and women of character. Give me the energy to provide them with a warm and loving atmosphere, to listen, not only with my ears but also with my eyes and heart. Remind me to pray for them daily, for their protection and for their walk with You. May I be a faithful parent, Lord, who asks You for wisdom and models the behavior of a Christ-follower, giving my children a hunger for You. May they know me as a person of prayer, with faith to move mountains. Lord, thank You for entrusting these children into my care. Amen.

SCRIPTURE FOR DEEPER INSIGHT

[1] John 12:49
[2] John 5:19
[3] 1 John 5:14
[4] John 4:24

REFLECTIONS

Have you been in a prayer group and had someone pray your thoughts? Consider this – perhaps the Holy Spirit confirms to you His will for the situation by giving someone else the words for your thoughts.

What is the last prompting you received from the Holy Spirit? How did you respond and what were the results?

If you don't sense the Holy Spirit, ask God to open your spirit to recognize His promptings. Then watch, wait and respond. He will answer.

Day Thirty-One

SEEDS OF HOPE

"Whoever sows bountifully will reap bountifully." 2 Corinthians 9:6

In the brokenness of life, I reached out to my sister, Sam. "My life is dead. Everything is dead; my marriage, my dreams, my passions. I am lost and without hope." Her response was priceless. "Mary, go buy some plant seeds, put them into the ground, and care for them. You need something to nurture." She was right. I focused on giving life as I checked the seeds daily, spending time ensuring they were watered, weeded, and properly spaced.

Years later, I met someone whose desire was to nurture life with aspirations far greater than plants. Patricia's childhood was bruised by abandonment, rejection and ridicule, yet along the way, the kindness of godly people pushed her forward. Her heart's ambition was to be an encouragement to wounded children by serving as a caseworker. She shared, "If I can plant a seed of hope in the life of a child during my one touch point, that will be enough." Her story challenged me to expand my nurturing skills from plants to people.

I asked God to increase my understanding of the reality of life among the poverty-stricken, or as scripture says, the least of these.[1] Being a single woman, I needed a group or ministry to tag along with, yet I was unaware how to orchestrate such an opportunity. Within days, I was invited to join a mission team headed to West Africa. The goal was to visit remote villages, meet with community elders to understand the needs of their people, and encourage them in the Christian faith. We visited areas whose housing consisted of dirt floors and thatch roofs, where restrooms were a hole in the ground, and the water source was a puddle of stagnant water. I prayed for the sick and elderly within the communities, and my emotions were stirred toward the dirty, yet content, children with wide smiles, sparkling eyes, and tattered clothing. Was there a way to plant a seed of hope in the life of just one of these children?

I asked the right question and soon understood the importance of child sponsorship through Christian organizations.[*] The cost is minimal to the giver, yet paramount to the child. As students age, they become high-risk for being sold into slavery to eliminate the expense of upbringing and education. Sponsorship provides the student with a uniform, meals, school supplies, and health care.

I decided to sponsor an eighth-grade girl, orphaned and living with her blind grandfather, who had no means of earning income. At first sight, she called me "Mama," and clung to me until we boarded the bus, hours later. The hardest part of saying hello was in saying goodbye.

A seed of hope and a future was planted in her life. My role? To nurture that seed through letters, monthly support and prayer. I trust God to grow her faith, and make sure she lives a purpose-filled life. "I planted the seed, another will water it, but God will make it grow."[2]

PRAYER

Father,

You created me with purpose, with a divine destiny to be fulfilled. Help me walk, day by day, in the steps leading to my purpose. Do not let my life on Earth be wasted time, but help me be intentional in strengthening my relationship with You and seeking Your presence. As I walk with You, give me the courage to take the necessary steps to break free from fear, strongholds, or selfishness. Let me not miss my next step. Please repeat it as often as it takes me to understand, and help me recognize the ways You confirm Your voice and promptings. Let my life make a difference for Your kingdom. Amen.

SCRIPTURE FOR DEEPER INSIGHT

[1] Matthew 25:40-45
[2] 1 Corinthians 3:6-9

* Note: If you are interested in sponsoring a child, check out these two organizations: www.internationalneeds.us/ or www.compassion.com/

REFLECTIONS

What seeds of hope have you planted lately?

Are you making a positive impact in the lives of those God places in your path?

Day Thirty-Two

THE HEART OF A PARENT

"Her children arise and call her blessed." Proverbs 31:28

The greatest gifts we can give our children, young and adult, are unconditional love and the example of a godly life. Do we miss the mark in both areas? Yes, and often. Yet, children tend to know the heart of their parents. They know when they are loved, and they know when a parent honors God. When one becomes a parent, it is time to put away selfishness and carefully consider how every choice and every decision will, in some way, impact the family. When mistakes happen, make amends and get back on track. Thus, the way of a godly parent.

When my children entered their high school years, they walked to their own beat, searching for identity among their peers, their adventures, interests, and opportunities involving temptation. The heart of a parent covers their children in prayer – for safety from violence, drugs, and people of bad influence. We love our children, guiding them as best we can, planting seeds of faith and wisdom along the way. However, there comes a time when their ear and heart no longer seek mom or dad for guidance. They look within to find their own way, or they look to others to direct their path.

As children find their way, with successes and hiccups, it is common for a parent to wonder, "Did I do enough to prepare them for adulthood?" It is also common to see adjustments needed within their relationships, lifestyle or character. For parents to continue having an influence on their adult children, suggestions must be in accordance with history, personality and relationship, as well as age-appropriate, respectful, and honoring boundaries. Once children become adults, they choose whom they will allow to influence their decisions, as they exercise their right to be independent in thinking, living, and beliefs.

As Christian parents, we know life will hit them with struggles, situations, and circumstances they will feel inadequate to handle. We know God is the answer when walking through the good and bad times. We have experience and understanding about God's grace, His provision, and His wisdom. We can always share the information when the opportunity presents, yet we know better than to force our faith on them. So, we release them to God, knowing their continued growth is their inward struggle and we must trust God's process of drawing them near.[1] We can neither fix their pain, nor can we reverse the clock to redo anything we may have missed when they were young. However, we can put our trust in the One who is most able to help our children build their personal relationship with Him and increase their faith,[2] as we continue to pray for them daily.

God is bigger than we can imagine, more loving than we comprehend, and able to direct the path of His children to see, know, and understand more of Him. As your children mature, pray they will be drawn to their Creator.

PRAYER

Father,

The children are grown, out of the house and finding their way. They know of You, yet in the depth of their being, they have not made the connection You are their personal and intimate God. No one can take them on this journey – they must seek You on their own. Lord, as their parent, my heart's desire is for my children to know and walk with You. This is where my faith is stretched. Just as You drew me, I trust You to draw them. You love them even more than I do. My continued role is to point them to You and pray for them. Be blessed, Lord, through the life and faith of my family. May I be faithful in praying for my children and releasing them to You to do Your work. Keep me from interfering where You are teaching and keep me from being their rescuer when You are orchestrating situations to draw them near. Increase my faith. Amen.

SCRIPTURE FOR DEEPER INSIGHT

[1] James 4:8
[2] Luke 17:5
[3] Romans 8:28

REFLECTIONS

What is your greatest concern about the children in your life?

If you are having difficulty forgiving yourself for decisions or choices made in the past that have negatively impacted your children, take a moment to seek God's forgiveness, and ask for grace to forgive yourself. Process through the disappointment with yourself by inviting God to work all things together for good.[3]

Write a prayer for your children, releasing anxiety and worry from your heart and placing them in God's able hands.

Day Thirty-Three

——— ◆◆◆◆◆ ———

GATHERING THE FRAGMENTS

"Wisdom is more precious than rubies." Proverbs 3:15

My life was fragmented. How did this happen? In search of significance, I had thrown away pieces of my identity to gain love and acceptance. Pieces were scattered in so many places, I didn't know if I could rebuild the original me and be made whole. At some point, pleasing others had taken priority over caring for Self.

Warning. People-pleasing is a trap that robs life, contentment, and freedom. This subtle trap lures its prey, guaranteeing unconditional love and security. This is a lie. God created each person as an *individual*. No two people are exactly alike. You are different, unique, and special.[1] You were designed and created by the Father of the Universe. Giving away your personal rights to gain unconditional love and acceptance are unnecessary. God loves you and He will bring people into your life who will encourage you, help you find your place, and love with great affection and respect.[2] It is never too late to gather the fragments and be made whole.[3]

How did God help me regain my shattered pieces? He sent me on a scavenger hunt to collect the scattered fragments. It has taken years to work through this list, and dare I say, the journey has been one of gaining wisdom, enjoyment and freedom. As you read through my list, begin formulating your own list of ways to regain any parts of your personhood that have been given away over the years.

- Find your voice. Lean into and express your opinions, thoughts, desires, and life stories.
- Rediscover your dreams from the past and for the present and the future.

- Find your goals. Work through a list of short-term, mid-term, and long-term goals, taking a step-by-step approach. It's okay to make mistakes or change your mind along the way.
- Find your laughter. Watch silly movies, hang with fun people, dance, sing karaoke. Discover new life-giving activities.
- Find new adventures. Take a road trip to a new place, walk across a swinging bridge, hike a mountain, try sushi.
- Create a bucket list. Include big and small things, expensive and inexpensive. Complete at least one per year. Revise, rewrite and extend your list annually.
- Find your strengths. Take a personality test to learn strengths and weaknesses. Engage in activities that take advantage of strengths. Work on growing through the weaknesses.
- Find your inner strength. Become a good steward of your life and all God has given. Exercise, eat healthy, get vices under control. Avoid negative self-talk, breathe through anxiety, trust God.
- Find community. Invest time in God and strong believers. Walk away from negative influencers.
- Find balance. Know what you can and cannot change. Overcome the want and desire to always be in charge.

PRAYER

Father,

Thank You for walking me through the maturity of life in all aspects. Give me emotional, spiritual and mental maturity. May I walk in the way You have set before me, not looking around to see what others are doing, but keeping my eyes on You. Reveal to me the areas of Self I have given to others and give me the courage and strength to gather the scattered pieces, so I may be whole. May I enjoy the journey of working through my scavenger list. You created me. I ask You to reveal to me who I am in truth, and how my identity is in You. Amen.

SCRIPTURE FOR DEEPER INSIGHT

[1] Psalm 139
[2] John 13:34-35
[3] 1 Thessalonians 5:23

REFLECTIONS

Use my list or create your own for gathering the fragments of your life. Journal your progress as you work through each step. Embrace Self and enjoy life.

Learn to set personal, then relational, boundaries. Decide whom you will, and will not, allow to speak into your life. Develop self-discipline, learn self-control. Discover yourself.

Day Thirty-Four

BREAKING STRONGHOLDS

"They laughed at Jesus." Luke 8:53

Mockery and ridicule can plant a seed of fear which, if watered through believing the spoken lies, grows into a tree producing the stronghold of people-pleasing. When Jesus visited the home of a dead girl, He told the mourners and wailers, "Stop wailing. She is not dead but asleep." The people laughed at Him, knowing the girl was already dead. The laughter stopped as Jesus took her by the hand, told her to "Get up," and she rose to her feet.

Oh, to be like Jesus, obeying God while disregarding the opinion of people.[1] More often we stand with the ones mocking and ridiculing. We sacrifice what we believe is best and blend into the crowd to gain approval, only to find a false sense of value. We trade our freedom of serving others for the servitude of people-pleasing. But we cannot serve two masters[2] and being a servant of the crowd influences our choice to turn from God.

The need to gain and maintain Man's approval leads to disappointment and failure. People-pleasers are trapped and carried into the slavery of serving human masters.[3] That master will never have enough, be happy enough, or carry their own responsibility. Instead, that master will find someone who needs the approval of Man and expect that man to carry the responsibility of making the master happy. They occasionally throw a morsel of approval and praise to satisfy their servant before increasing their demands and expectations. And the trap tightens its grip.

This trap was set against Jesus many times. In scripture,[4] as Jesus was preaching to a crowd, others tried to pull him away for selfish gain. Jesus would not allow Himself to be distracted from what God willed, regardless of who made the request. He had a backbone infused with obedience to

God.[5] Jesus allowed nothing and no one to trap him into any stronghold. His life was to prove and please God, not gain the approval of others.

How do we break free from this trap of being people-pleasers?

- Pray, "In the name of Jesus, I break this stronghold over my life."
- Pinpoint those sacrificial things done for other adults that are expected yet unappreciated. Learn to say "No." You are not responsible for the happiness of another adult. Refuse to feel guilty for saying "No." Stand your ground.
- Drop unhealthy expectations placed on others to make you happy or complete.
- Direct your life and happiness. Do not give control of your personhood to another. Take back the rein and become all God has purposed. Discover your value by knowing God. People-pleasing gives your power to others who use you for their own gain.
- Being a Christ-follower does not make you a doormat. Love God and others, speak truth, and walk in freedom. Become the person God designed you to be.

PRAYER

Father,

Today I pray for strength to cut the strongholds I have invited into my life, specifically that of being a people-pleaser. Your will is what I desire, not that of pleasing others who use me to fulfill their requests, carry their selfish burdens, and make them happy. Lead me, step by step, from the need to please others who have defined me in the past. Give me the courage to say "No" even though it may cause others to become angry or feel they are being inconvenienced. I no longer desire to sacrifice my life's call and purpose in favor of meeting the wants and desires of those who would seek to use me as a crutch. Help me care for myself, knowing it is not a sin to be a good steward of my body, soul and mind. Forgive me for giving away the rights to Self in unhealthy ways. Let me be a God-pleaser, which is the path to finding my significance. Amen.

SCRIPTURE FOR DEEPER INSIGHT

[1] John 2:23-25
[2] Matthew 6:24
[3] 2 Peter 2:19
[4] Luke 8:21
[5] Hebrews 5:8

REFLECTIONS

Are you a people-pleaser? If so, in what ways have you given away your personal power? How can you regain your power?

Consider reading the book, *"Boundaries"* by Henry Cloud.

Do you need freedom from other strongholds in your life? Here are a few to consider: Generational sin, unbelief, accusation, trauma, rejection, bitterness, envy, fear, addictions. For more information on overcoming spiritual strongholds, visit www.healingstreamsusa.org.

Day Thirty-Five

AMBUSH REVERSAL

"My power is made perfect in weakness."
2 Corinthians 12:9

I write and speak authentically and vulnerably, and I share life in the same way, trusting and believing people operate with good intent. Discernment is a gift that matures over time, often at the expense of learning through difficulty. In my speaking career, I am often faced with questions about my personal life. My thoughts, if someone asks a question, it is my role to answer honestly. Historically, I shared too much information, too quickly, trusting first and seeing motives in hindsight. I had a hard lesson to learn. People often attack others when they see a chink in the protective armor. In attacking, they step into Satan's plan of silencing God's messenger, using the ammunition of partial truth.

One morning, I awakened with a word of caution in my thoughts. "Fortify. Your weakness will be your downfall." I presumed the enemy was planning an ambush at an upcoming conference and I would need to be watchful. However, being watchful and fortifying are not the same. To be watchful is to be vigilant and alert. To fortify is to strengthen beforehand. In failing to understand the warning to "fortify," my weakness in discernment was used against me.

The conference was life-changing. God's message flowed into the hearts of the women. At the close of the event, I assumed the enemy had been routed. Before dismissing the final session, someone asked, "Mary, how can we pray for you?" I openly shared the reality of my marital situation, oblivious my honest answer would deploy the enemy. After prayer, I was pulled aside and cautioned, "When you shared your prayer request, I saw that you are ministering out of brokenness. You need to stop speaking until this has resolved." The ambush hit the target. Her words turned my focus from praising God to second-guessing His power. Was this true? Had I spoken out of brokenness and spread my distress among the women? When I inquired of the Lord, His answer hit home. "Not everyone is a safe place. Even some who proclaim to be Christ-followers fight to keep My words caged. Be vigilant, yes, but also be fortified by speaking only as I direct. 'Be wise as a serpent and harmless as a dove.'"[1]

God alerts us to oncoming danger and provides a way to safety. We each have areas of weakness to overcome. Scripture advises us to fortify those areas, which can include anything from lack of discernment to addictions. We are forewarned to submit our weakness to God, so He can provide the strength we need to withstand enemy attacks.[2] We are counseled to live by the Spirit and join our lives with Christ, so His characteristics replace our sinful nature.[3] Self-control is a by-product in following Christ. In the struggle to imitate Christ, we find eventual surrender to God, and strength to overcome the enemy's attempts to use our weakness as our downfall. We are to destroy strongholds keeping us from our purpose and submit to the Spirit to be made more like Christ. In doing this, the ambush of the enemy is reversed, and victory in the battle is claimed for God's Kingdom.

PRAYER

Lord,

Show me my weaknesses that need to be fortified. Help me stand firm amid adversity, knowing You whisper words of warning before the enemy attacks. May my ears and spirit be open to hear your warnings. Give me passion to know You within the depth of my being. I pray for tenacity to hold firmly to You, through thick and thin, belief and unbelief, joy and sorrow. Fortify me, Lord. Set me on the rock of Your foundation. May my faith and feet not be moved from understanding every battle is Yours, and You lead my every step. Amen.

SCRIPTURE FOR DEEPER INSIGHT

[1] Matthew 10:16
[2] 2 Corinthians 12:7-10
[3] Galatians 5:16-26

REFLECTIONS

How do you identify your weaknesses? These are the actions and attitudes which bring about remorse, conviction, or guilt; areas where you stumble in your faith walk. Beware, these same areas are openings in your protective armor the enemy will attack to bring destruction, silence you, embarrass or humble you in public.

Invite God into your obstacle or area of weakness. Ask for His help in overcoming and defeating the enemy attempts to use your weakness as your downfall.

Day Thirty-Six

FROM FEAR TO VICTORY

"The Lord is my Shepherd, I shall not want." Psalm 23:1

Standing in the security line at O'Hare International Airport found me in a puddle of fear. Not fear of flight, but a trace of social anxiety, coaxing me to forget the travel and return home. It was the first time returning to South Carolina since my world fell apart, and I was not ready to share my heartbreak with my extended family. Would they see me as a disappointment or a failure? Attending the high school graduation of my niece meant being surrounded by family and friends inquiring about my husband. Was I equipped to handle these questions in an honoring way?

The more I worried, the more anxiety beckoned me to run. Breathing deeply, I recited, "The Lord is my Shepherd."[1] I broke the phrase down, word for word, and repeated it different ways, putting the emphasis on a different word each time. I visualized the Lord as my Shepherd. He picked me up and cradled me in His arms. He stroked my hair and kissed my forehead. He whispered, "Everything is going to be all right. When you are afraid, lean into me. Put your head on my chest." My Shepherd and I made it through the security check and onto the plane. Seeing family and friends was healing, and my anxieties washed away as I realized the excitement of graduation was greater than my insecurities, and the world did not revolve around my emotional pain. Fear tried to take me down, but my Shepherd carried me through. The episode with anxiety exposed a fear of failure nestled within. Once exposed, faith stepped in to work through the process of healing.

Faith is the tool for digging deep in finding the root of emotional triggers, wounds and fears. When we trust God, we call on Him to walk us through the steps of healing. As He exposes brokenness within, we acknowledge and accept it, and invite Him to lead us on the pathway of self-discovery and overcoming fear. He walks us through our pain, holds us as we face past hurts and fears, and accompanies us through the stages of grief and healing.

I am amazed how God takes a tragedy in life and uses it to grow us more into His likeness. If we are willing to surrender our pain to Him and follow Him into the depth of our being so He can show us our brokenness, He brings healing in a way that is above anything we can ask or imagine. His desire is for us to be free. Free from the cage of fear, insecurity, insignificance, addiction, heartbreak, everything that hinders our lives from being all He has designed. I would never voluntarily walk into the brokenness and despair that came through the demise of my marriage. Yet, on the other side, after God's healing went into the depth of my soul, I can say, "What the enemy meant for harm, God has used for the saving of many lives."[2] In Him, we find freedom, release from oppression and inner darkness, and we come to know Him in a way we would not without the hardship we faced.

PRAYER

Father,

Thank You for life and health for me, for my family. Bring healing to our physical bodies. Place a hedge of protection around us, that our minds and bodies are protected from further negative impact. Touch us and bring healing to our innermost parts, our minds, our chemical balances, our bones, and bloodstream. Heal our emotions. Shine Your light in the dark places of the mind and bring peace. Give us the courage to see the deepest wounds within our Self and surrender those places to You for healing. Calm our anxious thoughts and still our fears. Let us release our burdens to You so we may find rest. May Your presence be the healing balm as You embrace us strongly with Your love. May we be of sound mind and thought, as we focus on You. Hold us steady and use us to speak words of healing to others. Amen.

SCRIPTURE FOR DEEPER INSIGHT

[1] Psalm 23:1
[2] Genesis 50:20

REFLECTIONS

Are there fears that hinder your growth or relationships with others? How can these fears be overcome to bring new life?

Remember to invite God into the healing process. He alone knows your complete history and the cause of all wounds and pain in your life. He knows the steps for your way forward.

Day Thirty-Seven

THE WAIT OF GOD

"Be still and know that He is God." Psalm 46:10

The important things of life and eternity are invisible to the naked eye. These include integrity, character, destiny, purpose and emotions. While we see things from our limited perspective, God sees and knows all. He is an orchestrator of people, time, places and events. He does everything with our best interest at heart. When we wait on His timing, we allow Him the opportunity to purposefully and masterfully work out the intricate details to fulfill His plan, both individually and corporately.

Unfortunately, we often grow frustrated in waiting for God to intervene in ways acceptable to our selfish plans, so we establish ourselves as god. We adopt the attitude of, "I will do it myself", leaving Him to watch us wave our wand of interference. Because of our microwave mentality, we push, manipulate, purchase or charm our will into existence. Then we find ourselves in situations we are not mentally or emotionally prepared to handle. We make messes that take longer to unravel than create.

We see an example of this in the book of Genesis.[1] In this story, Abram prayed, "Lord, you have given me no children, so a servant in my household will be my heir." The Lord replied, "A son coming from your own body will be your heir." Abram's wife, Sarai, grew impatient in waiting, so she stepped outside of God's plan to manipulate His promise.[2] She said to Abram, "The Lord has kept me from having children. Go, sleep with my maidservant; perhaps I can build a family through her." The maidservant became pregnant and birthed a son, whom they named Ishmael.[2] Sarai's plan not only caused resentment and bitterness within her own heart toward the maidservant and the child; it also caused problems to Abram's line of descendants for all time, affecting the future of the world.

After twenty-five years of waiting, God fulfilled His promise to Abram and Sarai by giving them a son, Isaac.[3] Why the long wait? Scripture says there is a time and season for everything and everyone. There is a time to be born and a time to die.[4] Isaac's birth was not merely for the enjoyment of Abram and Sarai in producing an heir and raising a child. Abram and Isaac were ancestors of Jesus. The timing of Isaac's birth was in alignment with every ancestor born between the time of Isaac and Jesus. God's timing plays a significant role in the history of the world and His Kingdom. When we wait on God's timing, we allow our life to come into alignment with His plan. Attempting to manipulate God creates friction and interferes with His best plan.

As we wait on God to work within our lives and fulfill His promises, may we be careful not to create our own "Ishmael." May we see "the wait" as God's supernatural way of orchestrating people, times, places and events to impact the world for His Kingdom.

PRAYER

My child,

Trust Me. I have not caused this shaking in your life, but I am here to guide you to a better place. Lean into Me and I will direct you step by step. Allow Me to lead. Do not fall into the temptation to go over, under or around My plan, which only leads to additional disappointment and disaster. My ways and timing are perfect. Though you cannot see the work I do, I am behind the scenes, preparing your next step. I develop and mature your character and replace your grief with joy. Allow Me to walk you through this chaotic time into a place of peace. I am trustworthy; I am faithful, and I am God, an ever-present help in your time of greatest need.

SCRIPTURE FOR DEEPER INSIGHT

[1] Genesis 15:3-6
[2] Genesis 16:15
[3] Genesis 21:5
[4] Ecclesiastes 3:1-2

[5] Lawson, J. Gilchrist. *Deeper Experiences of Famous Christians.* Anderson, IN: Warner Press, 1911.

REFLECTIONS

> *"Did you ever hear of anyone being much used for Christ who did not have some special waiting time, some complete upset of all his or her plans first? He knows best what will ripen and further His work in us."* Frances Ridley Havergal [5]

What are you waiting on the Lord to provide or answer? Are you tempted to go ahead of Him to find your own answer?

How have you gotten in God's way in the past by trying to "help Him" meet your needs?

Day Thirty-Eight

THE COMPANION OF PEACE

"Go in peace." Luke 8:46

When peace is disrupted, we have One who calms the storms of life, sits with us in our restlessness, and leads us into victory. Throughout this forty-day journey, you discovered peace-robbers and you prayed through pain and disbelief. Your prayers have reached the heart of the Lord, and His answer is on the way. Continue to lean into Him, lift your eyes and prayers, and wait in peace, knowing He is faithful. Jesus often spoke to those seeking His help, "Go in peace." He spoke these words to one He healed,[1] and repeated them to one He forgave.[2] God's peace is available to everyone, no matter the cause.

What interferes with inner peace?

- Being caught in the vortex of sin, cycling between regret and repeat, unable or unwilling to seek help in laying the sin aside in exchange for inner peace.
- Our behaviors, actions, attitudes, and motives; the need to control everything and everyone rather than releasing control to God. We only control ourselves and our reactions and interactions to situations and others.
- Idols of the heart. Instead of seeking the counsel of God for peace, we run to something or someone for comfort.
- Becoming caught in the turbulence of life, putting our focus on the crashing waves rather than the One who calms the storm.[3]
- Walking in disobedience, which brings unrest, regret, confusion, and worry.
- Lack of faith, lack of trust, and not knowing God.

What restores inner peace?

- Engaging faith to realize and remember, no matter what, God is in control. Faith has nothing to do with emotions or feelings.
- Walking in obedience, despite what our eyes see as reality. In the unseen spiritual realm, God watches, protects, and prepares the way ahead. He orchestrates time, resources, events, and people to meet the needs of His children. Keep praying, remembering 'God is faithful.'
- Being still before God, allowing His peace to overcome every emotion. Learning to 'be still' takes practice and patience. It's like going from the Charlotte Motor Speedway to the Bullock Creek Turtle Races. Time and activities come to a halt, the noise level decreases, and the overactive mind struggles to engage with the inner man, which is where we meet with God, spirit to Spirit.
- Practicing His peace by being in His presence, breathing in His goodness, and letting the worries and regrets rest in His hands. When we believe and trust His Word, our heart is at peace.

PRAYER

Lord, I need Your peace. Give me courage to surrender regret, shame, and anxiety. Help me trust You and walk in Your ways.

My child,
    I hold all things in My hand. My plans for you are good. My love is unconditional. Come, sit in My presence and allow Me to fill you with peace to carry you through the day. Your worries and difficulties are My miracles in the making. Go in peace.

SCRIPTURE FOR DEEPER INSIGHT

[1] Mark 24-34
[2] Luke 7:36-50
[3] Mark 5:35-41

REFLECTIONS

What activities or emotions rob you of inner peace? List them.

Rather than worrying or thinking about negative outcomes, journal your thoughts into a prayer.

Day Thirty-Nine

THE WAY FORWARD

"This is the way; walk in it." Isaiah 30:21

Dear Traveler,

Thank you for journeying through these forty days of prayer. May God's grace and guidance go before you, opening the way to greater understanding of who He is and who you are in Him.

Truly, He loves you with an everlasting love and He is always available for you when you call.[1] He loves the real you, the one hidden deep inside, known only to you. The warts, pimples and moles of your inner being others can't see. Don't be afraid to talk with Him about those things that bring embarrassment, humility, shame, or disgust. The healing comes when you admit your secrets and messes and ask Him for help.

There are things I prefer to hide from God because I don't want Him to be disappointed in me, or because I don't want to surrender them. In those things, He allows me to cycle, back and forth, until I am sick of them and willing to toss them. When the temptation comes to recover them from the trash heap, putting them back into my secret place of inner darkness, it doesn't take long before I remember the pain and angst they bring, and they are promptly returned to the trash pile.

Such is life. Such is humanity. It's the cycle of sin.[2] All experience it, battle it, strive to overcome it. Perfection doesn't come while we walk this Earth. There will always be something we struggle with.[3] I promise. I also promise you this - God is stronger than any struggle and temptation we face.[4]

Remember, He desires the best life for each of us. When we invite Him into our circumstances, He moves heaven and earth to come to our aid, to make Himself known to us, to rescue us from messes and put our feet on solid ground. He waits for us to call upon Him --- and as soon as we call,

He arrives. One of the beautiful ways of God is how He is always working on our behalf; He always has the answer to our needs in motion, and many times His work is undelivered because we fail to ask. Just as we don't want anyone forcing us into decisions we do not wish to make, He will not force Himself into our circumstances. He waits to be invited. So, continue to pray, continue to invite Him into every area of your life, and continue to give Him thanks for the work He does for you and those you love.

Keep pressing in to God and keep taking steps forward. You are loved. You are God's created one. You are His. Be encouraged!

"Now, it is God who makes us stand firm in Christ. He anointed us, set His seal of ownership on us, and put His spirit in our hearts as a deposit, guaranteeing what is to come."
2 Corinthians 1:21-22

PRAYER

Father,

You hold my life in the palm of Your hand. Hold me steady as I walk forward, step by step, into the destiny You have set before me. Give me courage and boldness to step outside my comfort zone and follow You in absolute obedience. May I walk in Your promises and Your way, knowing You are always with me. I love You Lord. Increase my faith. Amen.

SCRIPTURE FOR DEEPER INSIGHT

[1] Jeremiah 31:3
[2] Judges 2:11-12
[3] Romans 7:24-25
[4] 2 Corinthians 12:1-10

REFLECTIONS

Look back at your journaled responses. How have your prayers, goals and desires for this prayer journey been answered?

Ask God, "What is the next step in my way forward?" Listen to the inner voice, then journal your thoughts as they come into your mind. Was anything revealed you feel is your next step? Commit to follow through with it.

Consider working through this devotional again to mark and measure progress in your spiritual growth and way forward.

Day Forty

LIFE TO THE FULL

"I have come that they may have life and have it to the full." John 10:10

On the cross, Jesus bore the sins of the world, knowing the hardest punishment would be separation from God. There are two things to consider here. First, Jesus paid our debt by shedding His blood for our sin. Scripture says, "Without the shedding of blood, there is no forgiveness of sin."[1] When we are Christ-followers, our sin is covered by the blood of "the Lamb who takes away the sin of the world."[2]

Second, because Jesus willfully took responsibility for our sin, sins He did not commit, He suffered spiritual separation from God. Humanity projects blame for our wrongdoing to keep shame, guilt, and responsibility at bay. Jesus did the opposite. Rather than have humanity spiritually separated from the presence of God, He stepped into our guilt, shame and responsibility. His sacrifice meant, "I love you so much, I do not want you separated from the Father, for any reason, under any circumstance. I will pay the price for you." His death and resurrection cleared the way for the Holy Spirit to come and live within each believer.

I have been a believer for many years and have struggled with understanding the depth of the sacrifice of Christ for most of those years. Listed below are forty statements defining our faith. If you would like to extend this forty-day study, I suggest taking one statement per day, meditating on it, and journaling what it means to you. Scripture references are provided to further your study. Allowing a few minutes each day to study and meditate on one statement will open your heart and mind to deep truths about Jesus and your relationship with Him.

1	God created Man to be in relationship with Him.	Genesis 1:26
2	Man's life is physical, with a body, emotions, and desires.	Genesis 2:7
3	Man's life is spiritual. The spiritual is unseen.	1 Corinthians 2:11
4	The relationship between God and Man is spiritual.	John 4:24
5	God's presence and sin cannot co-exist. God is good. Sin is evil.	Habakkuk 1:13
6	The price for sin is death. It is evil.	Romans 6:23
7	Sin brings physical death, which is separation of the body and spirit.	Romans 5:12
8	Sin brings spiritual separation from God.	Isaiah 59:2
9	Man sinned. Sin is evil.	Genesis 3:17-19
10	Because God and sin cannot co-exist, Man's sin separated him from God.	Isaiah 59:2
11	Because the relationship between God and Man is spiritual, this is a spiritual separation.	Romans 5:12-14
12	Sin must be punished. It is evil.	2 Thessalonians 1:9
13	As punishment for sin, all people experience physical death, which is the separation of body and spirit. (Until the return of Christ)	Genesis 3:19 1 Thessalonians 4:17
14	God does not desire for man to experience spiritual separation from Him.	John 3:16
15	No person can enter God's presence without the forgiveness of sin.	Acts 2:38-39
16	God provided a substitute to take on the punishment for our sin.	John 1:29
17	God's substitute, His Only Son, Jesus, had no sin. Yet Jesus took on the sin of the world so Man could have forgiveness and Spiritual life with God.	2 Corinthians 5:21
18	When Jesus hung on the cross, all sins of all people, for all time, were laid on Jesus.	1 John 2:2
19	When the sins were placed in the body of Jesus, He was spiritually separated from God.	Matthew 27:46

20	Jesus died a physical death and suffered spiritual separation from God.	Matthew 27:50
21	Jesus' death on the cross brought freedom to Man from the guilt and penalty of sin.	Hebrews 9:14
22	All people sin. Man is born into a sinful world and no one is perfect. Therefore, we all need a Savior.	Romans 3:23
23	The substitute (Jesus) provided a way for God and Man to continue in relationship.	Ephesians 3:12
24	Forgiveness is available, but not automatic. We must humble ourselves and ask.	1 John 1:9
25	For salvation, we are told to "believe on the Lord Jesus Christ."	Acts 16:31
26	After the death of Jesus, God raised Him back to physical and spiritual life.	Luke 24:6-7
27	Jesus walked the earth for forty days and then He ascended into Heaven.	Luke 24:51
28	After Jesus departed, He sent the Holy Spirit.	John 16:7
29	Once we seek and receive forgiveness, the Holy Spirit takes residence in our Spirit and we are made new.	2 Corinthians 5:17
30	The Holy Spirit is our comfort, guide, teacher. He convicts of sin and draws us to God.	John 16:8-15
31	Once we receive the Holy Spirit, He is never removed from our lives.	2 Corinthians 1:22
32	Jesus is our example in how to live.	1 John 2:5
33	Jesus gives us understanding of God so we may know Him more. The Holy Spirit helps us walk as Jesus walked.	1 John 5:20 1 John 2:27
34	We can allow the Holy Spirit to increase in our life, or we can decrease His Spirit by living selfishly, ignoring His promptings, rebelling against His convictions, and moving forward without giving Him access to our heart and mind.	John 3:30-35

35	When we place our trust in Christ, we are guaranteed eternal life.	1 John 2:25
36	When our life on earth ends, we will be with God.	2 Corinthians 5:8
37	We are saved by faith, not by works.	Ephesians 2:8
38	We are to do good works out of love for God and others.	James 2:26
39	At the end of life, we will give account of what we have done in service to God in helping others.	2 Corinthians 5:9-10
40	Our hearts greatest desire, at the end of life, is to hear Jesus say, "Well done, good and faithful servant."	Matthew 25:23

PRAYER

Father,

My heart overflows with thanksgiving to You for making a way for the forgiveness of sin. May I daily remember to seek Your truth and Your ways. Thank you for sending Jesus to die in my place. Thank you for providing the cleansing I need to be free from the guilt and shame of the wrongs I have done. Give me greater understanding, Lord. Open my heart, mind and spirit to understand the depth of the gift of forgiveness, salvation and eternal life. Live fully in me, Lord. May my selfish will decrease, and may I have the courage to allow Your Holy Spirit to increase within me. Amen.

REFLECTIONS

Use this space to journal thoughts, write scripture, or pen prayers to God.

WORKS CITED

Unless otherwise noted, all scripture quotations are from the NIV.

The Bible. Zondervan NIV Life Application Study Bible. Grand Rapids: Zondervan, 1984.

Cowman, Mrs. Charles E. *Streams in the Desert.* Grand Rapids: Zondervan, 1997.

Lawson, J. Gilchrist. *Deeper Experiences of Famous Christians.* Anderson, Indiana: Warner Press, 1911.

Williamson, Marianne, https://www.brainyquote.com/authors/ marianne_williamson. Assessed 15 April 2019.

ABOUT THE AUTHOR

Mary Ethel Eckard is an author, speaker, and co-founder of Dragonfly Ministries, dedicated to the spiritual growth and encouragement of women. She travels internationally to speak and teach at women's conferences, workshops and retreats. She has a heart for teaching women how to connect with God and walk in His ways. Her captivating testimony chronicles a journey of relying on God's strength and guidance to navigate the storms and dark days of life, coming out on the other side with a greater maturity in and intimacy with Christ.

Mary's chief calling is to reflect God's light, joy, and love so others are drawn to Him, the source of life, as referenced in Matthew 5:16: "Let your light shine before men, that they may see your good deeds and praise your Father in heaven."

www.maryetheleckard.com

If you would like to schedule Mary to speak at your event, please contact her at admin@maryetheleckard.com or through her website, maryetheleckard.com.

Made in the USA
Coppell, TX
13 April 2024

31258921R00105